Praise for

This fabulous co...
cause the Chicks are scattered around the country,
have lived in an assortment of places, the recipes often
have a regional flare and variety. If you want your own
"killer collection of recipes," you'll love this book. Oh, and
while you're at it check out the Chicks and see if they are
cooking up some new mysteries!
—*Feathered Quill Reviews*

The kitchen is the ideal room in which to cook up the
perfect murder scheme. So mystery-themed cookbooks
are a natural. And this year's entry, The Cozy Chicks
Kitchen, is a no-brainer, given the ongoing popularity of
culinary cozies. The Cozy Chicks serve up a whole book's
worth of tempting treats, marvelous meals, sinful snacks,
and, of course, decadent desserts pulled from their own
novels. And even if they only pass through the kitchen to
use the phone to order out, cozy fans will enjoy the asides
and insights by the authors as they introduce their favorite recipes.
—*Mystery Scene Magazine*

Recipes from seven authors that offer a variety of delicious meals and snacks for you and your family to try.
With all the choices they offer, it's so hard to pick which
ones to try first, but when you do, you'll be glad you did.
Also, in the back of the book you'll find the list of con-
tributing authors, along with the book titles each has
available for purchase and their personal websites where
you can find out more about them. I'm so glad I stum-
bled across this cookbook because I've added a few new
recipes to my everyday cookbook that I use.
—*Night Owl Reviews*

This is a work of fiction. Names, characters, places, and incidents are either the product of the authors' imaginations, or are used fictitiously, and any resemblance to actual persons, living or dead, business establishments, events, or locales is purely coincidental.

Excerpt from *Icing on the Corpse* Copyright © 2001 by Mary Jane Maffini

Excerpt from *A Crafty Killing* Copyright © 2011 by Lorraine Bartlett

Excerpt from *The Busy Woman's Guide To Murder* Copyright © 2011 by Mary Jane Maffini

Except from *Scandals, Secrets And Murder* Copyright © 2014 by Maggie Sefton

Excerpt from *Murder in the Mystery Suite* Copyright © 2014 by Ellery Adams

Publisher's Note: The recipes contained in this book are to be followed exactly as written. The Cozy Chicks are not responsible for your specific health or allergy needs that may require medical supervision. The Cozy Chicks are not responsible for any adverse reactions to the recipes contained in this book.

We love our international readers too, so we have converted oven temperatures to Celsius and Gas Mark to make things a bit easier. However, please note all recipes were tested in Fahrenheit.

TEA TIME WITH THE COZY CHICKS

by The Cozy Chicks

Ellery Adams
Lorraine Bartlett
Duffy Brown
Kate Collins
Mary Kennedy
Mary Jane Maffini
Maggie Sefton
Leann Sweeney

Table of Contents

The Chicks' Fond Memories of Tea

Excerpts from some of our books

"Tea! Bless ordinary everyday afternoon tea!"
—**Agatha Christie**

INTRODUCTION

Dear Friends,

This book, *Tea Time with The Cozy Chicks*, is meant as an invitation to pull up a chair and join some of our fictional characters for a leisurely afternoon of sipping tea and sampling delicious treats.

As devoted readers of mystery novels, you already know what an important role food plays in our books. Characters gather around the table to discuss cases. They drink a staggering amount of caffeinated beverages and seem to be surrounded by an endless array of mouth-watering sandwiches, cookies, pastries, and chocolate. In short, these gals have a pretty good time, and we thought it would be fun to spend a little time in their world.

The result is *Tea Time With The Cozy Chicks*—filled with the lore of tea in so many of its incarnations, and an assortment of tea parties, menus and recipes included, and hosted by our characters. You'll find menu themes to cover life's major celebrations as well as those more intimate moments between close friends or romantic partners.

If you're worried about setting the perfect tea table because you aren't a professional pastry chef, floral arranger, or decorator, never fear. Neither are we. Hosting the perfect afternoon tea is about opening your home and your heart. You take care of that part and we'll help you with the rest.

And don't forget to turn to the end of this book. There, you'll find a list of additional tea themes as well as our complete bibliography of mystery novels and short stories.

The Cozy Chicks are always active on Facebook, so stop by and say hello. We'd love to see photos of how you made the tea menus from this book come to life, so feel free to share those on our wall.

Lastly, if you haven't visited our blog before, please pop by. It's a great way to get to know us and to catch a glimpse of the crazy life of a mystery writer.

And now…it's tea time!

The Cozy Chicks are …

Ellery Adams
Lorraine Bartlett
Duffy Brown
Kate Collins
Mary Kennedy
Mary Jane Maffini
Maggie Sefton
Leann Sweeney

Tea Time: History, Information, And Lore

"Tea to the English is really a picnic indoors."
—**Alice Walker**, *American author and activist*

A BRIEF HISTORY OF
AFTERNOON TEA
by Mary Kennedy

If you find your energy flagging in late afternoon and you yearn for a hot drink and a tasty snack, you're in good company. Anna, the 7th Duchess of Bedford, complained of having "that sinking feeling" every day and used to retire to her room with a pot of tea and a pastry or sandwich. As time went on, she began to invite her friends to join her and the custom of "afternoon tea" caught on. After all, in the early nineteenth century, most people only ate two meals a day, breakfast and dinner, so no wonder they had hunger pangs in mid-afternoon. Hot tea and a selection of pastries and sandwiches provided a nice pick-me-up and would carry them over until dinner, which was usually served at 8 pm.

Soon London hostesses followed her lead and drawing rooms were filled in late afternoon with women enjoying tea and sandwiches before heading out to Hyde Park for a promenade. It was the perfect opportunity to enjoy a quick snack with friends and catch up on the latest gossip before the traditional afternoon "walk."

Queen Victoria took the tea ritual to a new level when she began offering "tea receptions" to her guests. At these gatherings, usually held between 4 and 7 pm, as many as two hundred people would enjoy a delightful selection of finger sandwiches, scones, cakes and pastries. It was similar to our "open house" parties and guests were free to drop in as they pleased during those hours.

Nowadays, afternoon tea is still served in hotels and restaurants in England and is popular with tourists and Brits alike.

"A simple cup of tea is far from a simple matter."
—**Mary Lou Heiss**, *The Story of Tea: A Cultural History and Drinking Guide*

TEA TRIVIA
Collected by Leann Sweeney

All teas fall into four categories: black, green, white, and oolong.

Green tea is rich in antioxidants but can be bitter if iced and thus requires more sugar or other sweetener. It is best served hot.

Black tea, specifically orange pekoe, is the most common, but try Ceylon tea if you can find it. It has a very distinct and pleasant flavor.

Perfect tea is honey-hued and clear, NOT cloudy.

If you are having a tea party and want to make hot tea in quantity, make a concentrate ahead of time. When serving, put 2 tablespoons of concentrate into each cup then dilute with hot water.

To make concentrate, bring 1½ quarts of water to a boil. Soft water works best. Add ¼ pound of loose tea to the boiled water and steep for 5 to 7 minutes. Strain into a teapot.

Ice tea can cloud up easily, usually because of refrigeration. Add a little boiling water to clear it. It really is best kept at room temperature to keep it clear.

You may not know that both green and black teas were poured into the harbor at the biggest "tea party" of them all: the Boston Tea Party. The varieties are some you may never have heard of. According to historians 350 chests were dumped. The black tea varieties were Bohea, Congou and Souchong. The green were Singlo and Hyson.

"Drink your tea slowly and reverently, as if it is the axis on which the world earth revolves — slowly, evenly, without rushing toward the future. Live the actual moment. Only this moment is life."
—**Thich Nhat Hahn**, *Zen Buddhist Monk*

TEAS FOR YOUR GOOD HEALTH
By Kate Collins

GOOD NEWS FOR TEA DRINKERS
Research has now dispelled the old myth that tea dehydrates the body. Tea not only rehydrates as well as water does, but it can also boost the body's ability to fight some illnesses.

Impressively, tea has been linked to a variety of health benefits, including:

Reduced risk of heart disease and cancer

Improved insulin response and reduced blood sugar levels

Reduced pain and inflammation associated with rheumatoid arthritis

Reduced risk of dementia

Reduced glaucoma risk

Improved digestion

A study published in the *American Journal of Clinical Nutrition* in July 2008 found that caffeine from tea contains a natural protein called theanine that *counters* the normal side effects of caffeine, such as raised blood pressure, headaches and tiredness.

WHAT IS A TRUE TEA?
It is important to note that these benefits come from *true*

tea — green, black, and white — which are made from leaves of the tea plant, Camellia sinensis.

Herbal teas, which have been enjoyed since the days of ancient Egypt and China, are not true teas; they are actually tisanes, which means they are brewed from other plants. As they are produced by steeping dried or fresh flowers, fruits, leaves, seeds, and roots, they are known for reputed therapeutic effects.

CHAMOMILE AND PEPPERMINT

Diane McKay, Ph.D., from the Jean Mayer USDA Human Nutrition Research Center on Aging at Tufts University in Boston, and her colleagues at the school's Antioxidants Research Laboratory reviewed published studies of two popular herbal teas: chamomile and peppermint. Although there were no human trials on the calming effects of chamomile, they did find studies suggesting antimicrobial and antioxidant benefits from the tea, as well as signs of lowering cholesterol.

Chamomile tea should be steeped a little longer than other herbal teas in order to get all of the medicinal benefits. The petals of the tiny flowers are where the medicinal values lie.

Peppermint, long known for settling digestive upsets, has been shown to possess antioxidant and anti-tumor potential.

Mint is often used to:
• Reduce congestion in a cold or flu sufferer
• Reduce pain and bloating from gas
• Reduce cramping from diarrhea
• Act as a mild expectorant for a chest cold or bronchitis
• Induce sweating; the body's natural cooling mechanism. This is a natural way to reduce a fever
• Relieve nausea without vomiting.

A word of caution: If you suffer from acid reflux, min

tea may worsen your symptoms.

GINGER FOR COLD AND COUGHS
This ugly root is an ingredient in many natural cough, cold, and nausea treatments. Instead of drinking a glass of Ginger Ale that's loaded with high fructose corn syrup and artificial flavors, brew up a cup of ginger tea sweetened with honey. Your body will thank you.

CINNAMON FOR EVERYTHING!
Cinnamon tea is anti-bacterial, antiviral, and antifungal, making it an excellent all-around remedy. It has a whole host of immune-boosting antioxidants as well as being linked to lowered blood pressure. Cinnamon is one of the main ingredients in Chai tea.

BREWING HERBAL TEA
Steep the tea in a teapot with a lid or in a covered mug. This keeps all of the healing oils in the tea instead of evaporating. Most herbs should be steeped for about ten minutes for maximum results.

FIND THE BEST QUALITY GREEN TEA
With so many green teas on the market, you will want to find a high quality one. A sign of high quality is that it is in fact *green*, not brown. A brown colored green tea means it's probably oxidized, which can damage or destroy many of its most valuable compounds.

Japanese green tea brands are usually of a higher quality and have a lot less fluoride compared to Chinese green. Matcha tea is a vibrant bright green tea that contains the entire ground tea leaf, and can contain over *100 times* the beneficial proteins provided by regular brewed green tea.

Tulsi Tea is another healthy herbal choice, chock-full of antioxidants and hundreds of beneficial compounds known as phytochemicals. Phytochemicals are non-nutritive plant compounds that have protective and health promoting properties.

THE TAKEAWAY
There is a tea for everyone and there are a lot of reasons to drink them regularly. Besides providing health benefits, they're a natural, healthy alternative to sugary refreshments. Take tea and see!

Sources:
Mercola.Com:
http://articles.mercola.com/sites/articles/archive/2010/07/06/tea-healthier-drink-than-water.aspx
Rodale's Organic Life:
http://www.rodalesorganiclife.com/herbal-teas-under-microscope
The Organic Prepper:
http://www.theorganicprepper.ca/the-top-10-teas-for-your-herbal-medicine-cabinet-07242013

"If a man has no tea in him, he is incapable of understanding truth and beauty."
—**Japanese Proverb**

THE AMAZING MATCHA
by Kate Collins

Matcha green tea is a hot topic in the health and beauty sectors, mainly due to its potential health benefits. I've read so many good reports about it, in fact, that I decided to do some hands-on research.

My first task was to buy some, which turned out to be much more complicated than I thought. There is a plethora of matcha products on the market and I truly didn't know where to begin. So I began by reading up on it.

WHAT IT IS
Matcha is essentially processed green tea leaves that have been stone-ground into a delicate powder. The powder is then whisked with hot water until frothy. Because matcha is made from high-quality tea leaves, and the whole leaves are ingested, it's a more potent source of nutrients than steeped green tea.

WHAT THE CLAIMS ARE
In addition to providing small amounts of vitamins and minerals, matcha is rich in antioxidants called polyphenols that have been tied to protection against heart disease and cancer, as well as better blood sugar regulation, blood pressure reduction, and anti-aging. Another polyphenol in matcha called EGCG has been shown in some studies to boost metabolism and slow or halt the growth of cancer cells.

WHERE IT COMES FROM

Matcha leaves are grown in a number of places and, in fact, the practice of milling tea leaves into a fine powder and then whisking in water originated in China around the 10th century. But the best matcha comes from Japan, where it has been used in ceremonial preparations since the 12th century.

What most distinguishes matcha from other green teas is that matcha bushes are covered for up to 20 days prior to harvest to shade the leaves from direct sunlight. This is done to boost the plants' chlorophyll levels which then turns the leaves a darker, vibrant shade of green and increases the production of L-Theanine, an amino acid that occurs naturally in the tea plant and certain types of mushrooms.

One caution: Because you consume whole leaves in matcha, you may get three times as much caffeine as a cup of steeped tea, about the amount in a cup of brewed coffee. However, because of L-Theanine, you don't get the caffeine buzz of coffee. Instead, matcha supposedly creates an alert calmness that induces relaxation without drowsiness.

HOW IT'S PRODUCED

Workers pick only the best buds and, depending on whether the leaves are rolled out flat before drying or whether they are laid out to dry, will result in two different green teas. If the leaves are rolled out they become a premium green tea named Gyokuro, while the leaves that are laid out to dry become Tencha. Tencha is the leaf used for making matcha. Once the leaf is de-veined, de-stemmed, and stone-ground it becomes the fine powder known as matcha.

Matcha is usually made in two forms: usucha and koicha. Usucha translates to "thin tea," and is the most common preparation. This is what cafes and restaurants serve.

To prepare usucha, matcha powder is sifted into a bowl and whisked with hot water until frothy. The entire tea leaf is consumed in contrast to "regular" tea, which is a brewed beverage of processed tea leaves steeped in hot water. The matcha powder is whisked and suspended in the water. Let that bowl of matcha sit for too long and it will separate, unlike a brewed/steeped beverage.

Koicha means "thick tea." It's made with half the amount of water and twice the amount of matcha powder as usucha. The result is a very thick tea. Koicha is usually prepared during traditional tea ceremonies and is made from the highest quality of matcha powder, whereas usucha is made from the second highest grade of matcha powder.

WHAT ELSE YOU CAN DO WITH MATCHA

In addition to drinking matcha both warm and cold, there's no shortage of creative uses for the powder: infused into cocktails, whipped into lattes, dusted on savory dishes, and mixed into any number of sweets (such as ice cream, cookies and cakes). It has naturally sweet, grassy notes that make it adapt well to food and drink recipes.

MATCHA'S COST

Because of the laborious process required to produce matcha, the tea is generally pricier than others. Tea experts say that with matcha, quality is key, and quality comes at a price. Thus high quality, fresh, pure matcha is expensive. A low price tag can be a red flag for a poor quality product.

MY SUMMATION

I was a bit shocked at the price. I paid $24 for a small tin of ceremony quality, which I learned is better than culinary quality. However, a half teaspoon is all that is needed for a standard cup, so it will probably last a long time, especially because I'm not planning to drink more than a cup a day. It has a definite green grass flavor that I'll have to get used to, a lot more strength than the green tea bag I currently use. But the health claims sound promising, so matcha will become a permanent part of my tea collection.

Sources:
www.eater.com
www.news.health.com

"Rainy days should be spent at home with a cup of tea and a good book."
—**Bill Watterson**, *The Calvin and Hobbes Tenth Anniversary Book*

TEA PAIRINGS
by Duffy Brown

Wines aren't the only things to pair with foods. What about teas? Knowing which tea to serve with which food makes all the difference in the taste of the tea and the food served with it.

WHITE TEA
Because of the extremely subtle flavor of white teas, pair them with mildly seasoned rice, pasta, or potatoes.

GREEN TEA
In general, the subtle, vegetative flavor and aroma of most green tea is well suited to mild or subtly-flavored foods, such as seafood, rice, salads, melon, or chicken.

OOLONG TEA
Some say that the subtle flavor and aroma of oolong tea demands drinking it on its own. However, because oolongs can range between green and black teas, many can be paired with food along the same lines as the green or black teas. Greener oolongs tend to go well with scallops, lobster, a soup and sandwich, or sweet rich foods like deserts and fruits. Darker oolongs compliment somewhat stronger-flavored foods, such as duck, roasts, vegetable casserole, and grilled meats.

BLACK TEA

The more robust flavors and aromas of most black teas, as well as the most pronounced tannins, are well suited to pairing with full-flavored foods such as meat and spicy dishes, and pasta with sauce. Darjeeling tea is wonderful with egg dishes and creamy desserts. Keemun goes well with meats, fish, and Chinese, Mexican, Italian and Indian dishes. Yunnan pairs well with highly seasoned foods. Lapsang enhances the flavor of chicken, smoked salmon and lemony desserts Assam is best with hearty foods or breakfast foods.

PU-ERH TEA

Pu-erh teas are known for their digestive benefits. Not only do these teas pair well with meats and oily foods, they can offer a welcome settling effect after large, multi-course meals! Try a cup of Pu-erh after Thanksgiving Day or Christmas dinners. It's a perfect finish for a meal of red meat, stir-fry, or any oily foods.

CHOCOLATE AND TEA ... TWO FAVORITES COME TOGETHER!

Chocolate and tea are an excellent combination, if you know what tea to serve with which chocolate. Look for tea/chocolate pairings that share similar flavor characteristics and enhance one another. Or there are combinations where the flavors of the tea and chocolate contrast—these are sometimes the biggest hits. You can look for tea/chocolate pairings where the characteristics of each aren't necessarily the same, but are compatible or complimentary in some fashion as in two types of fruits, two spices, or two floras.

It is best to keep the tastes simple as too many added flavors (either in the tea or the chocolate) can make for pairings that are too busy or too complicated—and often not as enjoyable. Pick your focus and build around that.

Jasmine Green Tea or floral oolongs go well with dark chocolate that have a nuttiness, like almond bark or chocolates with a touch of peanut butter or walnut. Earl Grey black tea goes well with dark chocolate with a touch of citrus like orange, grapefruit, or even cranberry.

FLAVOR CONTRASTS

Earthy pu-erh teas go well with dark chocolates. Spicy teas, such as a robust black tea go with milk or white chocolate (think chai latte or chai mocha). Rich green teas, like Sencha green tea or even matcha green tea, also go well with milk or white chocolate.

COMPLEMENTARY FLAVORS

Teas with a roasted or "toasty" quality, such as houjicha green tea or wu yi oolong, are a good choice with chocolate caramels or mocha.

Assam black teas are delicious with milk or white chocolates that have a smooth cream filling. Lapsang souchong or similar smoked teas are best serves with really dark, bitter chocolate. Oolongs with sweet honey tones taste best with a citrus dark chocolate or chocolate infused with citrus. These are delightful and something a little different.

"What would the world do without tea! How did it exist? I am glad I was not born before tea."
—**Sydney Smith**, *wit, writer, and Anglican cleric*

TEAS AND TEA BLENDS
MADE YOUR WAY
by Duffy Brown

There are tons of tea flavors that you can buy in tea shops and at the grocery store, but there's a way to make tea just the way you want it.

You don't have to live in India, Japan, China, or some exotic place to grow tea. The Camellia sinensis (tea) plant can be grown in your garden, if you live in a warm climate, or can be grown in a container in your home. There's just one catch; it'll be three years before you can start harvesting leaves to make tea! If you are a patient soul, you should give this a try. I can't imagine anything more fun for a tea-lover. If you're like me you're thinking, "Gee, will I live that long?" So, here's another idea.

Consider creating your own herbal teas. True, herbal teas aren't "real" teas, but they're a great way to make tea with your own personal blend to suit your personal taste.

To make a tea blend, start with a good quality store-bought black, green tea or rooibos tea and add other ingredients like spices, dried citrus peels, and dried flowers.

Chamomile, lavender, and peppermint are three common herbal tea ingredients that are easy to buy or even grow in- or out-doors. Coriander, lemon bergamot, lemon balm, and jasmine are also popular tea herbs that can add interesting flavors and scents. Pretty much any culinary herb can be used in a tea.

You can experiment by combining herbs to create your own custom tea blends, suit your own taste, and even give as gifts. Here are just a few blend ideas to get you started:

Sometimes, the best tea is the simplest.

Plantain & Peppermint Tea
Ingredients
1 tablespoon organic plantain leaf
1 tablespoon organic peppermint leaf

Combine the herbs in a strainer, infuser, bag, or nest, and pour 1½ to 2 cups of boiling water over and allow to steep for 4 to 5 minutes.

SOME GREAT COMBINATIONS
Bergamot mint mixed with black tea makes a terrific Earl Grey. Sweet marjoram and chamomile is a nice match with some calendula petals sprinkled in for vibrant orange color. Rose hips, yarrow, and lavender add a bright floral tincture to any tea blend.

IF YOU WANT TO GET A LITTLE FANCIER, TRY THESE
Start with one cup of loose black, green or rooibos tea and add...

Floral Fantasy Tea
Ingredients
1 teaspoon lavender
1 teaspoon yarrow
½ teaspoon chamomile
½ teaspoon stevia

Spiced Anise Tea
Ingredients
2 teaspoons anise hyssop
¼ teaspoon cinnamon
¼ teaspoon vanilla bean
¼ teaspoon cloves

Devoted Remembrance Tea
Ingredients
2 teaspoons rosemary
2 teaspoons lavender
2 teaspoons marjoram
1 teaspoon anise hyssop

Dark Rose Tea
Ingredients
2 teaspoons rose hips
1 teaspoon anise hyssop
2 teaspoons yarrow
1 teaspoon bergamot mint

Aromatic Mint Tea
Ingredients
2 teaspoons spearmint
½ teaspoons marjoram
½ teaspoon sweet woodruff
½ teaspoon sage

When it comes to packaging, you can use pretty (and preferably light-proof) canisters or make your own teabags. There are "press-n-brew" tea bags where you add your tea blend and iron the opening shut. Ta-da … now you have your own personal teabag.

And here's another fun idea: once you get into making your own tea blends, try growing your own herbs and spices. In warmer climates, you can grow them outside.

In colder areas, try a windowsill herbal tea garden.

Use a south-facing windowsill and large well-drained pots of soil with lots of compost or fertilizer. Water only when the plant gets dried out (stick your finger into the soil up to your first knuckle; if dirt is damp and clings to your finger, don't water yet).

It's easy to convert a closet or dry basement into a mini drying room. Use clothes hangers with clamp clothespins to hold the herb bunches while they dry with a small fan circulating air.

The closet is great place to dry herbs since it's dark, warm, and dry. Mint, anise hyssop, yarrow, lavender, calendula, sweet marjoram, bergamot, chamomile, rosemary, and sage dry really well. Take the herbs down when dry as leaving them too long makes them dusty. Store the whole dried bunches in air-tight containers until ready to use. Strip the leaves and buds off the brittle stems and sort them in. Storing them in a plastic container is a good idea. Let the dried herbs—the leaves and buds—remain whole for as long as possible. You can take them off the stems during storage so the oils remain undisturbed. You should grind it up or crumple the herbs between your fingers just prior to use.

It's so much fun to make your own tea blends with friends. Figuring out favorite recipes make for the best tea parties ever.

"No matter where I serve my guests, they seem to like my kitchen best."
—**Unknown**

TEA TOWELS
by Lorraine Bartlett

I don't know about you, but I have a ton of linen souvenir tea towels from just about everywhere I've traveled. Okay, I didn't necessarily buy them, but I have them—either given to me by my late mother or late mother-in-law.

In years past, Mr. L was practically famous for always buying his mother a tea towel from every place in the US he went on vacation or business trips—and often in the guise of a hanging calendar. And when she downsized from a house to an apartment, his mother gave them to me.

No kidding—I must have 30-40 of them, ranging from the home where Charles Dickens was born, to Colonial Williamsburg, to Timbuktu, Ireland, Scotland, Wales, and beyond. I even have a Kirk and Spock Star Trek tea towel that was a Christmas gift from a friend (dated 1977). It's a little tattered by now, but still in the tea-towel rotation.

What's the fascination with tea towels? Well, they're useful. I use them every day in my kitchen, either for drying dishes (my dishwasher ALWAYS leaves puddles in the bottoms of mugs and glasses—and on my knives), or for just hand washing purposes. When I make tea sandwiches, I always place a damp tea towel over them so they don't go stale between the time I make them and put them on the table.

Tea towels (called dishcloths in the US) have a long history.

WHY LINEN?

What makes a linen tea towel so special? Well, it's soft—just perfect for drying gold-rimmed bone china cups, saucers, plates, and bon-bon dishes, crystal, and silver cutlery—and guaranteed not to scratch such finery.

"The best time to plan a book is while you're doing the dishes."

--Agatha Christie

Linen is made from the flax of linseed plants. As a kid, I remember seeing a demonstration at Upper Canada Village of a flax plant being thoroughly threshed or beaten or SOMETHING until it went from looking like a corn stalk into a palomino's golden blonde tail that was incredibly soft to the touch—and it was gorgeous to behold. They told us it would be made into linen. It was a lesson that I as an eight-year-old never forgot. These days, the fabric is more apt to be a blend of fibers, as linen is as delicate as the china it was meant to dry—and lint free, too!

In the early 20th century, American women made tea (or dish) towels out of feed or flour sacks. Though sturdy, they weren't exactly lovely to look at, so many were embroidered. (Feed sacks also came in cottons with prints that little girls coveted for their mothers to make pretty dresses, but that's another story.)

OTHER USES

In days of old, tea towels were also used as a kind of tea cozy, to wrap the teapot so that the tea would stay warm for a longer period of time. Lining a basket with a tea towel kept scones and rolls warm from the oven, too.

Vincent van Gogh never sold a painting during his lifetime, but he did a painting on a tea towel which eventually sold for over $3.5 million dollars. Yes—he painted on anything he could get his hands on—including a tea towel.

Now, aren't you glad you have a few tea towels to take care of your home and family?

Don't have any tea towels? Now would be a great time to start a collection. But don't just store them in your linen closet. Use and enjoy them!

"I always fear that creation will expire before teatime."
—Sydney Smith, *English wit, writer and Anglican cleric*

TASSEOGRAPHY: THE READING OF TEA LEAVES
For fun and maybe a little something extra...
by Duffy Brown

THE RITUAL
Put a pinch of tea leaves in the cup and pour boiling water over them, allowing them to stand about three minutes. Drink the contents of the cup, leaving tea leaves and a very small amount of liquid in the bottom.

The person whose fortune is to be told, called the "sitter," should take the cup by the handle, in the left hand with the rim upwards, and move it in a circle rapidly three times from left to right. Some of the tea leaves will seem to cling to the sides of the cup while others remain in the bottom. Next slowly turn the cup over onto the saucer and leave it there until all liquid drains away. Then set the cup back in the saucer.

The "sitter" should concentrate on his or her future destiny.

The handle of the cup represents the "sitter" in his or her own world and is the "south" point of the compass. The cup is divided into three parts. The rim is the present; the side equals the not far distant; and the bottom equals the distant future. The nearer the symbols appear to the handle, the sooner the event will unfold.

TELLING FORTUNES
The sitter gives the cup to the seer. The seer will see that the tea leaves are scattered over the cup in apparent confusion but it will be noted after concentration (or maybe a cup of spiked tea or two) that they form lines, circles, dots, small groups and figures.

Turn the cup and view from different angles until the

symbols become clear. Be patient and search carefully for symbols and note their position. The more you search (or drink the spiked tea) the clearer they become and they resemble various objects.

The symbols and their meanings:

ACORN—Continued health—improved health.

ANCHOR—Lucky symbol. Success in business or in love. If blurred or indistinct just the reverse.

HEART—A lover. If close to a ring, marriage to the present lover. If indistinct, the lover is fickle.

HEAVENLY BODIES—(Sun, Moon, Star) Good luck, great happiness, and success.

OWL—Indicates sickness or poverty. Warning against starting a new venture.

PALM TREE—Good omen. Success in any undertaking. Single people learn of marriage.

MOON (crescent)—Prosperity, fame. If cloudy, difficulties will be solved.

ELEPHANT—Good luck—good health—happiness (if they are pink you've had waaaaay too much of that spiked tea).

TRIANGLES—Unexpected good fortune.

BIRDS—Good Luck. If flying, good news from the direction it comes. If at rest, a fortunate journey.

Often the symbols are seen in groups; for example a bird and a heart with a letter N next to a palm tree might mean there is good fortune and a lover and much success, and the letter N is involved. And since the symbols are on the side of the cup, these are in the not too distant future.

— *Or* —

Fear not. In this teacup good fortune more than outweighs the bad. I see a marriage, possibly your own or a friend's. It seems certain that this good fortune is coming will be most unexpected.

The seer may have a "helper" to determine the shapes

as what the seer cannot see, often a helper does. Or the teacup can be passed around the circle of other tea drinkers to interpret the leaves.

Each symbol possesses some significance. Large or small determine their relative importance. For instance: if the likeness of a large sun is observed, it would mean that the sitter should expect some very good news indeed. If the sun is small, the good news is minor; but hey, good news is good news, right?

Direction of the symbol is also important. For example a bird flying toward the cup handle next to the letter means good news to the sitter from someone with that letter. A bird flying away from the handle means a letter from the sitter to someone of that name.

The small tea leaves frequently form lines. A line means a journey; a long line equals a long journey, etc. The direction of the journey may be determined by the direction of the line. If a line leads in the other direction, he or she is returning. A wavy or broken line means delayed journeys and straight-line quick journeys.

Dots surrounding a symbol indicate money in some form depending on the symbol. Should a leaf cling to the edge or rim of the cup, some event foretold by the symbols in the cup is imminent. Someone may be thinking of the sitter at the very moment. Look for a letter to find a clue to the identity of this person in the room. You will be amazed how often this is true!

Seeing the complete picture of the teacup as a whole often gives the seer a feeling of what is happening in the future, with good often outweighing the bad ... this is a tea party after all.

Have fun!

"A rose by any name would smell as sweet."
—**Shakespeare**, *Romeo and Juliet*

'TEA ROSE' FOR TWO?
by Kate Collins

When you order a bouquet of roses, you probably picture those long-stemmed beauties florists know as the hybrid tea rose. But before the hybrid came, there was simply the tea rose, so named for a fragrance reminiscent of tea leaves.

Tea roses date back to ancient Egypt and were imported from China at the beginning of the 19th century. They have some of the most sumptuous, elegant, and delicately colored blooms in the rose world. They are bushy, well-branched shrubs with pastel colored blooms that often look down.

Hybrid tea roses have been in cultivation since 1867 and are the most popular type of rose in the home garden. Considered a modern rose, they came about by crossing the hybrid perpetual rose and the tea rose to get the best features of both. They have a stiffer, upright growth habit and a brighter, more modern color.

Nearly all hybrid tea roses bloom repeatedly throughout the summer. They love sunshine and need a minimum of five hours to perform well. Morning sunshine is the best, with partial shading from the hottest afternoon sun. They are hardier than either the tea rose or the hybrid perpetual rose. Most of the hybrid teas have a mild to strong, lovely fragrance.

One of the reasons for the Hybrid tea rose's popularity as a gift is that the colors of long stemmed roses carry meanings passed down over the years.

Here is a list of some rose colors and their meanings:

Red — Love, Respect

Burgundy (and dark red) — Unconscious beauty or bashful

Light Pink — Admiration, Sympathy

Lavender — Symbol of enchantment. Lavender colored roses have also been used to express love at first sight.

Deep Pink — Gratitude, Appreciation

Yellow — Joy, Gladness

White — Innocence, Purity

Orange — Enthusiasm

Red & Yellow Blend — Joviality

Pale Blended Tones — Sociability, Friendship

Red Rosebuds — Purity

Rosebuds — Youth

Single Roses — Simplicity

Two Roses Wired Together — Coming marriage or engagement

NOT TO BE FORGOTTEN:

The Floribunda rose. This bush is a virtual blooming machine, with clusters of beautiful blooms at one time. Their blooms are similar to the hybrid tea rose or can have flat or cup shaped blooms.

The Floribunda rose bush makes a marvelous landscape plant due to its lower profile, ease of care, and hardy nature. Floribundas are also popular because they bloom almost continually during the season, as opposed to the Hybrid Tea, which blooms in cycles.

The Grandiflora rose is reported to have begun with a rose bush named Queen Elizabeth, a medium pink colored fragrant bloomer introduced around 1954. The Grandiflora is a cross between a hybrid tea rose and

Floribunda rose, picking up the best of both parents with beautiful blooms on long stems, hardiness, good repeat blooming, and cluster bloom production.

The Grandiflora rose bush likes to grow tall and will usually exceed all other roses in height. This rose loves the sunshine and also loves to be fed and watered well.

The Knock Out® rose bush is one of the most popular roses in North America, easy to grow and not requiring much care. These roses are also fairly disease resistant. Their bloom cycle is about every five to six weeks. The knockout roses are known as "self-cleaning" roses, so there is no real need to deadhead them. They are extremely heat tolerant, thus they will do well in the most sunny and hot of locations but need some winter protection.

Sources: http://www.gardeningknowhow.com/ornamental/flowers/roses/polyantha-floribunda-roses.htm

"Tea is the elixir of life."
—**Myoan Eisai**, *Kissa Yojoki How to Stay Healthy by Drinking Tea*

TEA TIME WITH THE DEAD
by Lorraine Bartlett

As odd as it may seem to us these days, the Victorians had a kind of romance with death.

Rural cemeteries were the precursor of today's parks, and were seen as a place to have tea—picnic style—with friends and family. Just spread out your blanket between the tombstones, brew a pot  of tea, and pass around the finger sandwiches and scones. They saw these cemeteries as "cities of the dead" and came to visit those near and dear to them on a regular basis. Not at all the way we look at one's final resting place these days.

Odder still, it wasn't at all unusual for the bereaved family to have their portraits taken of their dead in attitudes of repose. This was especially true when it came to the death of a beloved child. The mourning photo might be the only one taken of the recently deceased, who was often positioned on a chaise or chair to look as though they'd simply fallen asleep. This wasn't an aberration—it was an accepted custom in times when there was no penicillin to cure a simple infection, and the flu could become pandemic. It was a way for the family to never forget those forever lost to them.

One of the most beautiful rural cemeteries (and I've been there on numerous occasions, so I can attest to it) is Forest Lawn Cemetery in Buffalo, NY. This tranquil cemetery never fell into neglect and is the final resting place for such luminaries as Millard Fillmore (13th president of the United States, plus members of his extended family), Shirley Chisholm (the first African American woman to be elected to the House of Representative), and Grammy-Award-winning R&B and funk musician Rick James. It's also where the Frank Lloyd Wright Blue Sky Mausoleum was built beside a peaceful pond that's often filled with geese.

A teatime picnic in the cemetery was also described as "dinner alfresco." They were a thirsty lot and a multi-course meal was likely to include sherry to start, claret with the meat course, and champagne with dessert, with brandy to top it all off. That's in addition to ale, ginger beer, soda water, and lemonade served throughout the meal.

The meat course wasn't hotdogs or hamburgers, either. Such delicacies as lamb, roast fowl (take your pick of chicken, turkey, pheasant, duck, pigeon, etc.), ham, beef, or meat pies were on the bill of fare. Salad was popular, as well as sweetened stewed fruit with biscuits, puddings fresh fruit, cheese breads, rolls, butter and, of course—tea!

ANTIQUE TEA MEMORABILIA:
Notable Pieces Fetch High Brow Prices
by Ellery Adams

Tea is a beverage enjoyed by millions of people around the world. It crosses time zones, bridges culture gaps, and is often used to break the ice. People are extremely passionate when it comes to tea. They have their favorite brands and flavors, their favorite kettles, their favorite manner of steeping it, and of course, their favorite cup.

This passion for tea is hardly a modern concept. Man has been particular about his tea for hundreds of years. His devotion to this plant, and the drink made from its leaves, has only increased with time.

One of the oldest written records mentioning tea dates back to the 3rd century A.D. Since then, people have been steeping tea leaves in hot water and drinking pot after pot of the stuff.

It's no wonder that tea devotees around the globe decided to create beautiful vessels from which to enjoy their beloved beverage. Throughout the centuries and across cultures, tea sets and their accouterments have been fashioned using pottery, porcelain, sterling silver, glass, and more.

With such a widespread interest in the subject, it's no surprise that people began to collect tea memorabilia. These items include—but are not limited to—teapots, teacups, sugar bowls, cream jugs, caddies, trays, strainers, ball infusers, tins, spoons, and carts.

One might think that a simple teacup could only be worth so much money, but in 2014, a Ming Dynasty porcelain teacup sold at auction for $36 million in a bidding war that lasted less than seven minutes. The diminu-

tive cup, which was forged in imperial kilns and meas-
ures approximately three inches in diameter, is five hundred years old and purportedly one of only seventeen left
in the world. It has been dubbed "the chicken cup," because it is decorated with a rooster and a hen tending her
chicks. After the winning bidder swiped his American Express card two-dozen times to pay for his new treasure,
he took a ceremonial sip from the cup.

Very few collectors could afford to shell out that kind
of money for such a tiny item, but China isn't the only
country to have drawn record-breaking sales during an
auction containing lots of tea memorabilia. In 2011, a
pair of 18th century teapots called The Famille Rose
Teapots fetched an impressive $2.18 million during the
Bonham's auction in Glasgow, Scotland. The two white,
melon-shaped pots have enameled handles and spouts
and were painted with delicate plum blossoms.

Though not quite on the same pricing scale, a
chipped Wedgwood teapot from circa 1765 engraved
with a protest message of historical significance brought
an impressive $130,000. The message, "Success to trade in
America," is a direct protest against The Stamp Act and
foreshadows acts of rebellion by the American colonists
against The Crown (like The Boston Tea Party). The orange, egg-shaped teapot fetched forty times its estimate
at auction and was purchased by an American collector.

And of course, it's nearly impossible to discuss tea
memorabilia without mentioning collectibles made of
sterling silver. Nothing says elegance like a perfectly polished Tiffany & Co. sterling silver tea set. Now try to picture the individual pieces making a complete set and
you'll envision the teapot, coffee pot, creamer, sugar bowl,
waste bowl, hot milk jug, and a kettle on a lampstand.
Look closer at a particular example of Tiffany & Co. mag-
nificence. In this particular set, each piece is decorated
with intricately carved leaves and vines from which

golden fruit hangs. The fruit is actually comprised of an inlay of mixed metals including Japanese gold, copper, and platinum. And if that wasn't enough to impress, engraved dragonflies and butterflies flutter in-between and around the fruit and delicate foliage. This exquisite set, which comes on a matching tray, sold at a New York auction for $380,000 back in 2006.

As much as sterling silver dazzles, it failed to outshine Meissen porcelain when claiming the top spot as far as auction prices go. Mention the term, 'Half-Figure Service,' to any self-respecting porcelain collector and they will nod their head in appreciation, for this tea service sold at auction in London in 2012 for a whopping £541,250 (approximately $840,000). The name 'half-figure' comes from the type of decoration found on the set. Half-length figures were painted on each piece in the Meissen factory near Dresden. The multi-cultured figures, which have been painted in remarkable detail, are engaged in various activities. On one plate, a man is leading a horse, and on another plate of the same size, a different man is leading a camel. The only thing missing from this incredible set, which was made circa 1723 and consists of tiny tea bowls, beakers, saucers, a milk jug, a sugar bowl, and a hexagonal tea canister with lid, is the teapot itself. Imagine the price it would have brought at auction had the set come with its original teapot!

Thin, nearly translucent porcelain tea sets like the splendid Meissen "Half-Figure" service were often produced for decorative purposes alone, and while such items can fetch high prices at auction, some collectors focus on tea memorabilia that was actually used. For them, part of the passion in collecting these objects is the knowledge that people made cups of tea with these items. Hands touched these things over and over again in order to enjoy a hot cuppa, and sometimes, the beauty of a collectible is in knowing how many lives it has touched.

Antique tea balls and tea spout strainers are smaller collectibles with a large market. These useful objects can have a wide range in price, but can easily climb into the hundreds of dollars if made of sterling silver by a known silversmith. For example, a Gorham sterling tea ball with ornate chasing and piercing and a Gorham mark and date (1894) could sell for $600. A sterling tea spout strainer from Tiffany & Co. with tiny piercings might bring around $400 in today's market.

Finally, one cannot discuss tea memorabilia without mentioning tea caddies. These range in size and material from wood to silver to metal. One could collect only fruit-shaped caddies such as an antique Japanese aubergine tea caddy made of stained hardwood. A lovely little gem like this could set one back over $4,000. Or, if a tea caddy that locks and has its own key is more appealing, a wooden pear-shaped caddy with a hinged lid could cost over $5,000. And if fruit-shaped, barrel-shaped, tent-topped, urn-shaped, or plain rectangular tea caddies aren't special enough, there are some special antique caddies on stands available for the discerning collector. A circa 1820 rosewood tea caddy with stand with bone handles, velvet lining, and a maker's stamp might bring close to $9,000 in today's market.

Despite the impressive—and often daunting—dollar amounts listed in this article, tea memorabilia is available at such a wide price range that there are objects for sale to fit everyone's budget. For buying sources, look beyond eBay and try out rubylane.com or register to bid at a number of live auctions across the world at liveauction-eers.com. Who knows how that sterling silver wild rose tea strainer you buy today will appreciate ten years from now? Or how a friend will cherish the gift of a beautiful Staffordshire purple aster teacup and saucer? Or a family member would delight over starting his or her own collection after receiving an English walnut tea caddy with geometric inlay?

Regardless of the object, tea memorabilia is loved and appreciated by millions. This is undoubtedly because tea is loved and appreciated by millions. As long as there are tea leaves to steep, there will be tea items to buy. Why not start your own collection today?

I wish you many hours of pleasant sipping and happy treasure hunting!

"Come, let us have some tea and continue to talk about happy things."
—**Chaim Potok**, *American Jewish author and rabbi*

COZY CHICKS TEA TIME FUN FACTS

It doesn't matter what kind of tea you like, they all come from the Camellia Sinensis plant.

~~~

There may be as many as 1500 varieties of tea.

~~~

A lot of people confuse afternoon tea (sometimes known as low tea) with high tea. Historically, afternoon tea was considered a dainty "ladies" social affair and served on low tables (aka, a low tea), whereas high tea was served at a regular-height table and the food on offer for the working classes was more robust in nature. Items that might be served for such a heavy meal were meat pies (think steak-and-kidney), fish, crumpets, vegetables, potato or onion cakes—all washed down with tea.

~~~

Some studies seem to indicate that black tea may have cardiovascular benefits and orange pekoe is actually a black tea. Good for the heart? How romantic is that at a (possible) engagement tea?

~~~

Got warts? The tannic acid in black tea is said to help remove them.

~~~

While it's said that loose leaves make the best tea, approximately 96% of all cups of tea served around the world are made with teabags, which were invented in the US in the early 1800s to hold samples of teas brought from India.

~~~

Did you know that tea is often used as a household cleaner? Many people use black tea to keep their hardwood floors looking shiny and lustrous. The tannic acid in the tea can help restore a dull floor. It's always a good idea to spot test first. And let's not forget about green tea. This tea is a terrific odor eliminator. Is there a funky smell lurking in your refrigerator? Just place a spoonful of green tea leaves in a bowl in your refrigerator and the leaves will absorb the nasty odors in no time. That's the magic of tea!

~~~

Besides being delicious, raspberry tea is full of vitamins and antioxidants, but even better, it's good for tummy troubles, in case any teddies or kiddies are suffering from them.

~~~

Though tourism is India's #1 industry, the cultivation of tea comes in second. And though tea originated in China, it's Indian tea that is most commonly drunk throughout the world

~~~

Since 1987, the official White House brand of tea hails from South Carolina—the only state that has a major tea plantation in the US. It's called American Classic.

~~~

Where do you find the most tea drinkers in the US? The South and Northeast.

~~~

In the 20th Century, *Tea For Two* was the second most performed song. Happy Birthday came in first. (Source: the US Society of Composers, Authors and Publishers.)

~~~

In Russia, tea is made in a samovar, which can keep the tea hot for hours. (They're also commonly used in Iran and Turkey.)

~~~

In Iran and Afghanistan, tea is considered to be the national beverage.

~~~

In China, black tea is called "red" tea.

~~~

Don't ask for "chai" tea in India, Russia, and many other countries. The word "chai" literally means "tea." (You wouldn't want to ask for "tea tea.")

~~~

Earl Grey tea is flavored with the bergamot orange rind and was named after the second Earl Grey, British Prime Minister 1830-1834. It's likely the Earl Grey blend of tea developed to avert the chronic tea shipment shortages from China.

~~~

The holiday season can be really stressful because there's always so much to do. Luckily, we have tea! Did you know that black tea contains an amino acid called L-theanine, which helps you to relax? That's right! Black tea reduces your stress levels and has calming effects. It's the perfect beverage for a hectic time, so brew yourself a pot, put your feet up, and grab a cozy mystery to read. Go on, you deserve a break.

~~~

Tea every day may keep the dentist away. Tea helps fight cavities.

~~~

While the Brits drink about 165 million cups of tea a day (that's 62 billion cups per year), they are only the second-largest nation of tea drinkers per capita. The Irish come in first. (Bewley's anyone?)

~~~

The tea plant is an evergreen, but keep it trimmed. Without pruning, it can grow over thirty feet tall.

~~~

Get out the umbrella! Tea plants need a minimum of 50 inches of rain every year.

~~~

Tea carts (or tea trollies as they are known in the UK) are simply a rolling shelf from which to serve tea. They usually consist of two shelves to house the tea service and refreshments and have been around since the early 19th century. Many's the Victorian home that boasted such a piece of furniture which were used to impress guests. A vase of flowers often accompanied the dainty sandwiches and cakes, and, of course, a beautiful teapot to top it all off.

~~~

Fun Facts!

~~~

Chintz China may just be the epitome of teatime dishware. Many patterns abound, but all have a common motif: myriad flowers similar to chintz textile patterns. The heyday of this glorious transferware was between the 1920s-1960s. Royal Winton Potteries in Stoke on Trent, England, were said to be the originators of this often-imitated dishware, but Shelley Potteries churned out many patterns, too. Some of the more famous patterns are Summertime, Hazel, Sunshine, and Julia. Chintzware is always cheerful—a perpetual garden in bloom. What could be better?

~~~

While 519+ million pounds of tea are imported into the US every year, an estimated 85% of that tea is consumed as iced tea.

~~~

To keep your loose tea or tea bags from absorbing moisture, store them in a sealed jar or tin.

~~~

Reuse your tea leaves (if using tea bags, discard the bags) by adding them to the soil of your houseplants (or add them to the compost pile). Roses seem to thrive on them!

~~~

Can't find clotted cream? Make your own Devonshire Cream!

Ingredients
1 3-ounce package of cream cheese, softened
1 tablespoon confectioner's sugar
½ teaspoon vanilla extract
½ cup heavy (whipping) cream

Beat the cream cheese until it's light and fluffy. Beat in the sugar and vanilla. Gradually beat in enough of the cream to a spreadable consistency. Do not overbeat. Cover and chill for at least two hours.

Yield: 1 cup

~~~

Tea Dying: Want to age lace, sheets, t-shirts, pillowcases or other materials? An easy way to do that is with tea! Here's what you need:
A large pot to boil water
Tea bags (black tea works best)
Tongs, wooden spoon, or chopstick
White Vinegar

How-to:
Boil a large pot of water. Add 4-5 teabags (more if you want your material dyed a richer color of brown). Turn off the heat and let the tea steep for 10 to 20 minutes. Remove the tea bags.

Submerge your fabric in the hot tea water. Swish it around with the spoon or chopstick, and let it soak for an hour or more. (The longer it soaks, the darker the color.)

To set the color, add in ½ to 1 cup of white (clear) vinegar.

Wash/rinse — and voila! You've got a lovely tea-stained doily, shirt, or whatever to be proud of!

Make It Fun!

"Tea ... is a religion of the art of life."
—**Okakura Kakuzō**, *The Book of Tea*

IDEAS TO PERK UP
YOUR PLACE SETTINGS
by Mary Jane Maffini

- Pick up vintage linens at yard sales and thrift shops — they don't need to match!
- Make small posies: peonies, violet, daisies or any other traditional blooms from the garden. To showcase them, I use simple vases or even little jam jars at each place setting for a casual feel.

- Find vintage cake or serving plates, which are easy to spot at flea markets and garage sales. Tiered cake stands make a beautiful impression. Don't forget the cake knife, too!
- Serve tea in several real teapots with different tea blends in each.
- Using pretty serving plates makes everything look and taste better.
- A selection of linen or other cloth napkins will bring out the color in your plates and make guests feel special. Instructions for folding them into interesting shapes can be found by searching online. (Search for: standing fan; bishop's hat; the pyramid; the bird of paradise; the arrow, etc.)
   Adding a bit of soft background music will add am-

biance. How about a chamber quartet, soft jazz, or new age music?

•   Name cards at each place setting set an elegant tone. Here's an idea; bake cut-out cookies and ice them with each guest's name.

"Surely a pretty woman never looks prettier than when making tea."
—**Mary Elizabeth Braddon**, *Lady Audley's Secret*

FUN THINGS TO WEAR TO A TEA
by Mary Jane Maffini

Society is pretty casual these days, but a tea party can give us a chance to dress up a bit, either from head to toe, or by choosing just one special item to give us a lift.

Here are some diverse ideas to consider. You might want to pick one (or more), or you can also add your own!

- Pearls; one, two, or even three strands!
- A little black dress and pearls (very Audrey H!)
- A gauzy summer scarf in a pastel print
- Your grandmother's crystal drop earrings
- A long flowy skirt or a short skirt with a big flower
- A floppy straw hat with a ribbon
- Your mother's charm bracelet
- Flowers in your hair
- A pink hat with a perky little veil
- Bangles
- Cocktail rings
- Kitten heels or ballerina flats

- A boa or knitted (fluffy) scarf
- Vintage gloves, especially white
- Crystal beaded necklace
- A fascinator (hat)
- Silver jewelry

"You can serve high tea around the dining room table, but afternoon tea is more of a living room occasion, with everything brought in on a tray or a cart."
—**Angela Hynes**, *The Pleasures of Afternoon Tea*

A BAKER'S DOZEN OF
DREAM-WORTHY TEA ROOMS
By Mary Jane Maffini

Fiona Silk, from my own comic capers series, *Lament for a Lounge Lizard* and *Too Hot to Handle,* can't really get out of town on a holiday. She's usually either the subject of a police investigation or attempting to save a friend from life in a cold and lonely cell. And, of course, she doesn't have two cents to rub together. As she's a failed romance writer with no sex life (coincidence?), until she wins a lottery, she'll have to merely daydream about the perfect tearoom in the perfect location in the perfect city. These suggested tea rooms are really dream-worthy spots and serve marvelous teas. Let's hope Fiona keeps buying those lottery tickets. Would you like to dream along with her?

UNITED KINGDOM
The National Gallery Tea Room, *London, UK.* Can you picture yourself gazing over Trafalgar Square as you savor your afternoon tea here? Perhaps you'll be wearing a hat.
The Pump Room Restaurant, *Bath, UK.*
This popular and elegant destination is always full and

lively, an essential stop in a tour of the fascinating ancient city.

Chawton House, *Hampshire, UK*. Jane Austen did much of her writing in this historic home. Now Chawton House is a perfect spot for an afternoon tea. Who knows when Mr. Darcy might drop by?

The Palace of Holyroodhouse, *Edinburgh, UK*. The Queen's official residence in Scotland offers a sumptuous afternoon tea, with a champagne variation too. Maybe two lottery tickets, Fiona?

CANADA

The Fairmont Chateau Laurier, *Ottawa, Ontario*. Less than a block from Canada's Parliament buildings and  with a matching green copper roof and elegant carved granite exterior, Zoe's restaurant offers an elegant and stylish tea experience. Perhaps a Prime Minister will whisk by, too.

The Fairmont Empress Hotel, *Victoria, British Columbia*. A person can step into the past and enjoy the sumptuous traditional tea in this grand historic hotel. Well worth the three thousand mile trip for Fiona.

The Prince of Wales Hotel, *Niagara-On-The-Lake, Ontario*. This beautiful village on the Niagara River sees thousands of visitors a year and part of the appeal is the beautiful tea at this lovely hotel. Antiques and oil paintings lend a genteel feel. The food is wonderful—especially those jasmine tea infused raisins in their world-famous scones.

UNITED STATES

The Russian Tea Room, *New York, NY*. What a majestic New York experience and with tea and atmosphere! Fiona should really switch to champagne for a once in a lifetime experience.

The King's Carriage House, *New York, NY.* What a spot to sit back and sip, savoring the dramatic background of those red walls while enjoying the trappings of royalty with tea.

The Rose Garden Tea Room, *Huntington Library, San Marino, CA.* Imagine enjoying a delicious and sumptuous tea while surrounded by three acres of roses in this spectacular garden setting.

The Brown Palace Hotel, *Denver, CO.* The elegant lobby is the setting for afternoon tea in this historical landmark, where patrons enjoy their finger sandwiches while a harpist or pianist plays for their enjoyment.

The Grand Hotel, *Mackinac Island, MI.* For more than 100 years, a sumptuous tea has been served in the parlor of this magnificent hotel, with the lilting tones of a chamber group of musicians.

AUSTRALIA

Sydney Harbour High Tea Cruise, *Sydney, NSW.* While

sailing on one of the world's most beautiful harbours, enjoy a sweet or savory high tea along with the spectacular view.

Tea Time And Recipes

"Under certain circumstances there are few hours in life more agreeable than the hour dedicated to the ceremony known as afternoon tea."
—**Henry James**, *American writer*

A PROPER YORKSHIRE TEA
by Mary Kennedy

MENU
Cucumber Finger Sandwiches
Yorkshire Scones
Oatmeal Crispies
Lemon Drizzle Cake
Lincoln Ginger Biscuits
Victorian Sponge Cake

INTRODUCTION
Rose Harper: "When I discovered that Ali and Taylor's (from the Dream Club Mysteries) ancestors lived in the north of England, Minerva and I came up with the idea of hosting a proper Yorkshire tea. Minerva and I may have our differences, (I prefer Yorkshire Gold tea and she loves English Breakfast tea), but one thing we can agree on—this menu is sure to please!"

Minerva Harper: "I was thrilled that Rose's research turned up Ali and Taylor's British roots. Ali and Taylor have been so kind, providing all the treats for the Dream Club meetings. We thought it would be fun to host a special evening for everyone. We had the tea party at our house and it gave us a chance to use some lovely china tea cups in floral patterns. We decided to use a heather-and-cream color scheme for our tablecloth and napkins. Cut glass vases with sprigs of lavender completed the tablescape. If you closed your eyes, you could almost imagine you were standing on the Yorkshire Moors, gazing out over the North Sea."

THE TABLE

Taylor Blake: The Harper sisters arrived in late afternoon, when the back patio was at its most lovely, shaded by Banyan trees. Rose brought her favorite Wedgwood tea service, Wild Strawberry, and I noticed the teapot was cradled in a handmade mint green cozy. Almost all of us prefer Yorkshire Gold Tea, but Minerva added a Wedgwood Sterling Coffee Pot filled with fragrant Hazelnut Supreme for the coffee fans in the group.

After Minerva arranged the cups and saucers, she quickly spread a vintage hand-embroidered tablecloth over one of our outdoor tables. It was creamy white linen with a border of tiny tea roses and she placed a stack of matching napkins next to it. Meanwhile, Rose arranged some freshly cut pink roses in a cut glass vase, the perfect centerpiece for an afternoon tea. Then she stacked Wedgwood Signet Platinum desert plates, along with Georgian Rose Sterling Silver flatware, one of my favorite designs. The total effect was simple and elegant, perfect for our first Dream Club tea party. I could hardly wait for the club members to arrive.

THE TEA
Taylors of Harrogate Yorkshire Tea

DON'T FORGET THE FLOWERS
Abby Knight, from Kate Collins' Flower Shop Mysteries, says....

"England is the most garden-loving country in the world, with more gardens open to the public than anywhere else, and some of the most spectacular are the large castle gardens in York. One such garden is the Yorkshire Lavender Farm situated in the Howardian Hills. As the name implies, it is known for its stunning array of lavender, with flowers in white, pinks, blues, lilacs and magnificent deep lavender purples with a range of distinct and heady scents."

A Bloomers Flower Shop arrangement for a proper Yorkshire Tea would include:

Flowers
Lavender stems in white and lilac
Anemone (anemone blanda) in pink
White roses
Green and white hydrangeas
Yellow ranunculus.

Container
A pottery/ceramic water pitcher—one-handled or two—with or without a design on it.

RECIPES

Cucumber Finger sandwiches.
Ingredients
24 slices thin white bread
2 chilled, thinly sliced cucumbers
12 ounces cream cheese, softened
Salt and pepper
Spread a slice of bread with cream cheese and top with sliced cucumber. Sprinkle with salt and pepper. Top with another slice of bread, trim the crusts, and cut into quarters. (Repeat 11 times.)

Yield 12 servings, or 48 triangle sandwiches

Yorkshire Scones
Ingredients
3 cups all-purpose flour
1 tablespoon baking powder
1 cup (2 sticks) butter, softened at room temperature
¼ cup, plus 2 tablespoons, granulated sugar
3 eggs
1/3 cup of milk (You may need to add a couple more tablespoons of milk to get the dough to stick together)
½ cup of raisins. (You can substitute dried cranberries, chopped dates, or a mixture of all three.)

Preheat the oven to 350°F (180°C, Gas Mark 4). Sift together the flour and baking powder. In a separate bowl, beat the butter until creamy. Add the sugar, beating until pale and fluffy. Add the eggs, one at a time, then add the flour mixture and the milk. Sprinkle the raisins over the dough and gently fold them in. Drop by "mounds" onto a baking sheet. Bake for 20 minutes or until golden brown.

Yield: 12 scones

Lemon Drizzle Cake
Cake ingredients
3 large eggs
1 1/3 cup self-rising flour
1 cup granulated sugar
6 ounces (¾ cup) butter
zest of two fresh lemons
Glaze ingredients
juice of two fresh lemons (the ones you zested)
1 cup confectioner's sugar

Preheat the oven to 350°F (180°C, Gas Mark 4). Grease a loaf pan. Cream together the cake ingredients until they form a nice smooth batter. Pour the batter into the pan and bake for 30 to 35 minutes, or until a toothpick comes out clean. To make the glaze, mix the fresh lemon juice with the confectioner's sugar. Poke holes in the cooked cake with a thin skewer. Make sure the holes go all the way down to the bottom of the cake. Carefully pour the lemon glaze over the cake.

Yield: 12 servings

Lincoln Ginger Biscuits
Ingredients:
¾ cup butter, softened
1 cup granulated sugar
1 egg
¼ cup molasses
2¼ cups all-purpose flour
2 teaspoons ginger
1 teaspoon baking soda
¾ teaspoon cinnamon
½ teaspoon ground cloves
¼ teaspoon salt
¼ cup additional sugar

Preheat the oven to 350°F (180°C, Gas Mark 4). Cream the butter and sugar together. Add the egg and molasses and mix well. Place the flour, ginger, baking soda, cinnamon, cloves, and salt in a separate bowl and mix well. Add the flour mixture gradually to the creamed mixture and mix well. Roll into balls and then roll into the additional sugar and bake for 10 to 12 minutes on cookie sheets.

Yield: 30 cookies

Victorian Sponge Cake

Ingredients
6 ounces (¾ cup) butter
1 cup granulated sugar
3 eggs
1 1/3 cups self-rising flour
raspberry jam
1 pint whipping cream, whipped (optional)
jar of lemon curd (optional)

Preheat the oven to 350°F (180°C, Gas Mark 4). Grease the bottom of two round cake baking pans. Cream the butter with the sugar until light and fluffy. Beat the eggs then add to the mixture, beating well after each addition. Gently fold the flour into the mixture. Do not overbeat. Divide equally between the two prepared cake pans. Bake for 25 minutes. When the cakes are cool, remove them from baking pans. Spread raspberry jam on one cake, top with whipped cream (if desired), and then top it with the other cake. Another option is to use lemon curd as a filling.

Yield: 10 slices

"But indeed I would rather have nothing but tea."
—**Jane Austen**, *Mansfield Park*

A BON VOYAGE TEA PARTY
by Duffy Brown

MENU
Chantilly's Pecan Nut Cups
Elsie Abbott's Cucumber Soup
Reagan's Yummy Cornbread
Gloria Summerside's Chicken Salad Delights
Walker Boone's Perfect Compote
Annie Fritz Abbott's Praline Pumpkin Pie
Auntie KiKi's Party martini
Auntie KiKi's It's a three-olive-problem Martini

It's a Bon Voyage Tea Party for...
Auntie KiKi
Sunday noon
At Reagan Summerside's
Prissy Fox Consignment Shop
To help Auntie KiKi and Uncle Putter get
around in Europe...
Please bring a phrase or two in a foreign language to share

INTRODUCTION
Reagan Summerside here from the Consignment Shop Mystery series. I'm having a *Bon Voyage Tea Party* for my dear Auntie KiKi. She and Uncle Putter have booked a whirlwind trip to Europe. To make sure Auntie KiKi does not forget us back here in Savannah I'm serving up some true Southern dishes that are the favorites of her best friends.

INVITATIONS

I'm inviting ten of Auntie KiKi's closest friends. I went to VistaPrint.com where they have great invitations for a Tea Party or for a Bon Voyage themed party. They are inexpensive, and I can get them quickly. I just plug in the information I want on the invitations and the work is done for me.

I also want everyone to teach Auntie KiKi how to say "Hello" and "Good-bye" and "I live in Savannah," in various European languages to get into the spirit of the party...and in case my dear auntie gets lost, knowing these phrases will get her back to us. I'll put this information on the invitation as well.

DECORATIONS

Places like Party Cheap online has international picks to stick in my little sandwiches and matching plates to give the party a Bon Voyage flair. I'll get little toy airplanes and put them around the red, white and blue flower arrangement for the center of the table and the buffet table.

THE TABLE

I'll use a white tablecloth and white napkins tied with red and blue ribbon and a little international flags stuck into the bow.

I have two teapots and will borrow six more and serve up eight teas from around the world. I'll buy ten different and adorable cups and saucers for the guests to use at the party. They can then take them home as a thank you gift for coming to the party and as a remembrance. I'll have the tea at the buffet table with little cards stating the type of tea and food on the table to be passed once everyone is seated.

I like music when guests arrive, and the theme being international, I'll play something Italian, French and

Spanish. To get things started off on the right foot when the guests arrive, everyone gets one of Auntie KiKi's signature martinis listed below.

RECIPES

Gloria Summerside's Chicken Salad Delights
Ingredients
½ cup flaked coconut
½ cup chopped walnuts
½ cup green grapes sliced
1 (8-ounce) package cream cheese, softened
2 tablespoons mango chutney
1½ teaspoons curry powder
¼ teaspoon salt
¼ teaspoon pepper
2 cups diced cooked chicken
18 white bread slices
3 tablespoons diced green onions
mayonnaise

Toast the coconut and walnuts in shallow baking pans at 350°F (180°C, Gas Mark 4), stirring occasionally, 5 to 10 minutes or until golden brown. Spread the mayonnaise on one side of each piece of bread. Stir together the cream cheese and next 4 ingredients; gently stir in the chicken. Spread evenly on bread slices mayo side in. Sprinkle evenly with the coconut, walnuts, and green onions. Top with bread. Trim the crusts, and cut diagonally.

Yield: 36 triangle sandwiches

Elsie Abbott's Cucumber Soup
Ingredients
2 cups chicken bouillon
2 cups skim milk

1 cup sour cream
2 large cucumbers, peeled and minced
½ cup chopped green pepper
2 teaspoons dry mustard
2 tablespoons instant onion soup mix
2 tablespoons dried parsley
½ teaspoon dried dill
½ teaspoon salt
1 tablespoon paprika
fresh parsley for garnish

Combine all the ingredients in a blender and mix well. Chill for 4 hours or longer and serve in chilled soup cups. Top with parsley as a garnish.

Yield: 10 ½-cup portions of soup

Reagan's Yummy Cornbread
(Make in a cast iron skillet)
Ingredients
1¼ cups coarsely ground cornmeal
¾ cup all-purpose flour
¼ cup granulated sugar
1 teaspoons kosher salt
2 teaspoons baking powder
½ teaspoon baking soda
1/3 cup whole milk
1 cup buttermilk
2 eggs, lightly beaten
7 tablespoons unsalted butter, melted
2 strips of bacon

Preheat the oven to 425°F (220°C, Gas Mark 7) and place a 9-inch cast iron skillet inside to heat while you make the batter. Fry the bacon and reserve the drippings. In a large bowl, whisk together the cornmeal, flour, sugar, salt, baking powder, and baking soda. Whisk in the milk, buttermilk, eggs, and butter.

Carefully remove the hot skillet from the oven. Reduce the oven temperature to 375°F (190°C, Gas Mark 5). Brush the bottom and sides of the hot skillet with the bacon drippings. (I never said this would be healthy.) Pour the batter into the skillet and place it in the center of the oven. Bake until the center is firm and a cake tester or toothpick inserted into the center comes out clean, 20 to 25 minutes. Allow to cool for 10 to 15 minutes and serve.

Yield: 8 to 10 slices

Chantilly's Pecan Nut Cups
Crust
½ cup butter
3 ounces (9 tablespoons) cream cheese at room temperature
1 cup all-purpose flour

Cream the butter and cheese. Blend in the flour. Chill on hour. Shape into 24 balls. Press the dough into small muffin tins that have been treated with cooking spray.

Filling
1 egg
¾ cup light brown sugar
1 tablespoon butter, melted
1 teaspoon vanilla extract
2/3 cup pecan pieces

Preheat the oven to 325°F (170°C, Gas Mark 3). Beat together all the ingredients until smooth. Fill each shell 2/3 full. Bake for 25 minutes. Cool and remove from the pan. Top with whipped cream.

Yield: 24 small muffin cups

Walker Boone's Perfect Compote
Ingredients
2 tart apples (such as Granny Smith), grated
2 pears, grated
2 oranges, diced
2 banana, diced
1 cup strawberries fresh
1 can apricots, drained and chopped
½ cup orange juice
2 tablespoons lemon juice
8 tablespoons granulated sugar
1 cup white wine

Combine the first six ingredients in large bowl. Sprinkle
with the orange and lemon juice. Add sugar and wine.
Mix and keep at room temperature for 2 hours. Chill for
four hours. Use a slotted spoon for serving to drain off
liquid.

Yield: Makes ten ½ cup servings or twenty ¼ cup servings

Annie Fritz Abbott's Praline Pumpkin Pie
Crust
1 unbaked 9" pie shell
1/3 cup ground pecans
1/3 cup brown sugar
2 tablespoons of butter, softened

Preheat the oven to 450°F (230°C, Gas Mark 8). Combine
the pecans, brown sugar, and butter. Press into a pie shell.
Bake for ten minutes.

Filling
3 eggs beaten

1 cup canned pumpkin
2/3 cup brown sugar, firmly packed
1 tablespoon of all-purpose flour
¼ teaspoon ground cloves
¼ teaspoon allspice
½ teaspoon salt
½ teaspoon ginger
½ teaspoon cinnamon
1 cup evaporated milk

Mix all the filling ingredients together until smooth and creamy. Add the filling to the partially baked pie crust and bake at 325°F (170°C, Gas Mark 3) for another 40 minutes.

Yield: Makes one 9-inch pie

Auntie KiKi's Party martini
Ingredients
1½ ounces vodka (the good stuff)
2 ounces triple sec
1 teaspoon superfine sugar
3/4 ounce freshly squeezed lemon juice

Mix vodka, triple sec, sugar and lemon juice in a cocktail shaker half filled with ice cubes. Shake well to make sure sugar is blended. Pour strained liquor into a sugar-rimmed martini glass and garnish with a twisted peel of lemon.

NOTE: To create a sugar-rimmed glass, take a lemon wedge and rub the drinking surface of the glass so it is barely moist. Dip the edge of the glass into sugar.

Yield: 1 martini

Auntie KiKi's It's a three-olive-problem Martini
Ingredients
1 ounce dry vermouth (the good stuff)
cracked ice
3 pimento-stuffed green olives on a toothpick
4 ounces gin (more of the good stuff)

Fill a metal shaker with cracked ice. Pour in the dry vermouth and stir for five seconds. Add the gin and stir briskly for 10 seconds, strain into a chilled cocktail glass and garnish with the olives.

Yield: 1 martini

"Wouldn't it be dreadful to live in a country where they didn't have tea?"
—**Noël Coward**, *English playwright, composer, director, actor and singer*

CHOCOLATE LOVER'S TEA
by Kate Collins

MENU
Finger sandwiches
Red Pepper and Goat Cheese
Snappy Egg Salad
Crunchy Munchie Veggie

Small Cakes
Pecan Pie Delight Bites
Peanut Butter and Chocolate Squares
Chocolate Cherry Brownies

Scones
Hurry Up Cinnamon Pecan Scones

On the table
Raspberries and fresh cream
Sugar and milk

The Teas
English Breakfast & Chocolate Coconut

You are cordially invited to
Bloomers Flower Shop's
Chocolate Lovers' Tea Party
Time: 2-4 p.m. Wednesday afternoon
Place: Bloomers coffee-and-tea parlor
Dressy-casual attire suggested.
Abby Knight, *proprietor*

Dear Friends,

My assistant Grace Bingham, a UK native, will be hosting our event, and she's pulling out all the stops. Our white, wrought-iron ice cream tables will be given the royal treatment with tablecloths of French Chantilly lace, rose pink linen napkins, Grace's own Chantilly rose patterned Royal Doulton china teapot, teacups and saucers, and a beautiful three-tiered cake server.

And what a delightful menu she has planned. Finger sandwiches for the top tier, cakes on the second and her famous scones on the third. Naturally all of these tasty offerings will either include chocolate or compliment it, even the teas. They are: Coconut Cocoa, Tulsi Vanilla Crème, Green Moroccan Mint, Coconut Rum Tropical Green, and Grace's standard English Breakfast.

The staff here at Bloomers wishes you a delightful afternoon of chocolate, tea, and conversation. You might even want to stop by my display case in the shop to purchase some of the gorgeous Chantilly roses featured in the table centerpieces.

Cheers!
Abby

DON'T FORGET THE FLOWERS
For this tea, Abby Knight would most certainly use chocolate cosmos because of their chocolate scent. The *cosmos atrosanguineus* is a deep maroon, velvety flower (sometimes almost black) with dark brown centers on long, slender, reddish brown stems. This perennial native of Mexico resembles a daisy, blooms from early summer to autumn, can be overwintered indoors if grown in a northern climate, and makes good cut flowers.

The arrangement would include:
Flowers
Chocolate cosmos

Pale yellow buttercups
Orange button mums
White tulips (in season) or white roses
Mint stems for greenery
Container: An empty cocoa canister or a cookie jar would make the perfect vase.

RECIPES

FINGER SANDWICHES
Nutty Red Pepper and Goat Cheese
Ingredients
2 ounces soft goat cheese
1 ounce (3 tablespoons) cream cheese or Neufchatel cheese
arugula
fresh basil leaves, whole
roasted red peppers cut into strips (or ready made from jar)
6 slices soft bread, crusts removed
1 cup finely chopped walnuts

Mix the cheeses and spread on 3 slices of bread. Layer the arugula, basil leaves, and red pepper strips and finish with the remaining 3 slices of bread. Cut each sandwich into 4 triangles. Roll the sides of each triangle in chopped walnuts.

Yield: 12 finger-sized servings.

Snappy Egg Salad
Ingredients
6 hard-boiled eggs
½ cup olive oil mayonnaise
¼ cup spicy brown mustard
1 tablespoon lemon juice

¼ teaspoon hot sauce
1 tablespoon chopped sweet pickles or pickle relish
1 avocado, finely chopped
sea salt, black pepper
6 slices dense bread, crusts removed

Mash the eggs in a large bowl; stir in the mayonnaise, mustard, lemon juice and pickles. Carefully fold in avocado. Season with salt, pepper, and hot sauce to taste. Divide the egg salad among half the slices and spread on the bread. (Add leaf lettuce for some crunch.) Top with the remaining bread. Trim the crusts. Cut into triangles.

Yield: 12 finger-sized servings.

Crunchy Munchie Veggie Sandwich
Ingredients
1 10-ounce carton hummus, plain
1 small jar Greek olive (Kalamata) tapenade or your favorite olive flavor
¼ cucumber, diced
1 medium carrot, coarsely grated
6 slices whole grain bread, crusts removed

Mix all ingredients together and spread on 3 slices of the bread. Top with the remaining bread and cut each sandwich into 4 triangles. (Option: Hummus with olive tapenade may be substituted for first 2 ingredients.)

Yield: 12 finger-sized servings.

LITTLE CAKES
Pecan Pie Delight Bites
Ingredients
1 15-ounce package yellow cake mix
½ cup melted butter

4 eggs
2 cups chopped pecans
½ cup brown sugar or coconut
    sugar
½ cup dark corn syrup
¾ cup natural maple syrup
(or use 1¼ cup maple syrup
and omit the corn syrup)
1 teaspoon vanilla
½ cup semisweet chocolate chips (optional)

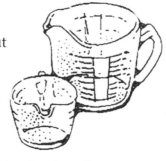

Preheat the oven to 350°F (180°C, Gas Mark 4). Grease the bottom and sides of a 13 x 9-inch pan. Reserve 2/3 cup of the dry cake mix for the filling. In a large bowl, combine the remaining dry cake mix, butter, and 1 egg. Mix until crumbly. Press into the pan. Bake for 15 minutes.

Combine the reserved cake mix, sugar, syrups, vanilla, and 3 eggs. Beat at medium speed for 1 to 2 minutes. Pour the mixture over the crust. Sprinkle with pecans. You can also sprinkle with chocolate chips for even more flavor. Bake 30 to 35 minutes or until set. Cut into bite-sized squares.

Yield: 4 dozen small bites.

Peanut Butter and Chocolate Chip Squares
Ingredients
½ cup natural peanut butter*, no added sugar (*you can substitute almond butter)
½ cup butter
2 eggs
¾ cup packed brown sugar or coconut sugar
½ cup sugar or coconut sugar
½ teaspoon vanilla
2 ¼ cups unsifted all-purpose flour or almond flour

1 teaspoon baking soda
½ teaspoon sea salt
1 12-ounce package semisweet chocolate chips

Preheat the oven to 350° F (180°C, Gas Mark 4). Coat 13 x 9-inch pan with cooking spray. Cream the first 6 ingredients. Combine the flour, baking soda, and salt. Add the flour mix to the cream mixture. Stir in the chocolate chips and spread in the pan. Bake for 25 to 30 minutes. Cut into bite-sized squares.

Yield: 3 dozen

Chocolate Cherry Brownies
Ingredients
1 15-ounce box chocolate cake mix
1 21-ounce can cherry pie filling
2 eggs
1 teaspoon almond extract

Frosting
1 cup sugar or coconut sugar
1/3 cup milk or coconut milk
5 tablespoons butter
1 cup semisweet chocolate chips

Preheat the oven to 375° F (190°C, Gas Mark 5). Mix the first 4 ingredients; pour into a greased 15 x 10-inch jelly roll pan. Bake 20 to 30 minutes.

Frosting: In a pan, heat to boiling: sugar, butter, and milk. Boil for 1 minute. Add the chocolate chips and stir until melted. Pour over the warm bars. Cut into bite-sized squares.
Yield: 4 dozen squares

Hurry-Up Cinnamon Pecan Scones
Ingredients
3 cups all-purpose flour or almond flour
2/3 cup granulated sugar or coconut sugar
1 tablespoon baking powder
2 teaspoons ground cinnamon
½ teaspoon salt
¾ cup cold unsalted butter, cut into pieces
1½ cups chopped pecans (can be toasted for additional flavor)
1 large egg
1 cup whipping cream
1 teaspoon vanilla extract
Parchment paper

Topping:
2 tablespoons whipping cream
1 tablespoon granulated sugar or coconut sugar

Preheat the oven to 425°F (220°C, Gas Mark 7). Stir together in a large bowl flour, sugar, baking powder, cinnamon, and salt. Cut in the butter with a butter knife or pastry blender until crumbly. Stir in pecans.

Whisk together egg, 1 cup cream, and vanilla; using a fork, add to the dry ingredients until the mix forms a rough dough. Using an ice cream scoop or a 1/3 cup measuring cup, drop onto parchment paper-lined baking sheets. Brush tops with cream. Sprinkle with sugar. Bake for 18 minutes or until browned. Serve warm.

Yield: 14 servings

"A woman is like a tea bag; you can't tell how strong she is until you put her in hot water."
—**Eleanor Roosevelt**, *American First Lady and activist*

A BACHELORETTE TEA
by Duffy Brown

The Menu
Rudy's Stuffed Cherry Tomatoes
The Mustang Lounge's Chicken Liver
    Spread
Irish Donna's Orange Muffins
Fiona's Tea Party Punch
Irma's Easy Melon and Berry Surprise
Evie's Cheesecake

Guess who's getting married?
It's a Bachelorette Tea Party for
Irma Sutter
Sunday noon
The front porch of the Grand Hotel
Mackinac Island
No gifts as your friendship is the best
gift of all.
Please bring:
Twenty bags of your favorite tea to share
and your favorite teapot to show off

INTRODUCTION
Evie Bloomfield here from the Cycle Path Mysteries set on Mackinac Island. A dear friend's getting married and want to throw her a bachelorette party. She's a woman of a certain age, so going to Vegas, doing Jell-O shots, and ogling male strippers just doesn't work, but a Bachelorette Tea is perfect and it can also serve as a luncheon.

DECORATIONS
It's spring on Mackinac Island and I'll decorate with pink and white. I'll use flowers as centerpieces and I'll set them around the room to add to the ambiance.

I'll use a white tablecloth with pink napkins tied with pink-and-white silk flowers. These are inexpensive at any discount store. I'll wrap the stem around the napkin. Easy and colorful and it adds to the flower theme.

I like to have music when the ladies first arrive. Johann Strauss II *Voices of Spring* and Walt Mendelssohn's *Spring Song* along with Beatles *Good Day Sunshine, Here Comes the Sun,* and *I'll Follow the Sun* all work well.

When guests first arrive, I'll serve Fiona's Tea Party Punch listed below. It's a great way to get everyone chatting and relaxed...especially if you add the vodka.

SEATING
We'll sit at one large table that will seat every one comfortably. I'll have a buffet table set up with all the lovely teas and little note cards by each pot where the guests can print the type of tea inside.

TABLE SETTINGS
I'll have pink and white votive candles for atmosphere. At the buffet table I'll have the geraniums in pots with impatiens to fill in.

The food will be served on pretty dishes I already have or can find at the local thrift stores, which usually have a nice selection on sale. This allows the guests to fill their teacups and select the food after they are seated. No need to juggle so many plates at the buffet table. I'll use my grandmother's china; it's not expensive, but I love the little roses around the edge. I'll have cups and saucers by the teapots and the little salad plates with the napkins at the table.

DON'T FORGET THE FLOWERS

Abby Knight, from Kate Collins' Flower Shop Mysteries, says....

Single women out for an afternoon or night of fun, laughter, and a little frivolity—this is what she sees for a Bachelorette Tea:

Flowers

Fleur Primeur — a special tea rose that is white on the outside and vivid pink inside. This beauty is from France. Ooh-la-la!

Dancing Lady Orchid — fun and bright in yellow

"Kissproof" lily in deep pink

Maidenhair fern for greenery

Containers

Enough tall iced tea glasses for every guest. One stem of each flower per glass. If using clear glass, fill bottom with glass marbles. Group glasses in the center of the table, or in clusters on multiple tables, and hand them out at the end of the event.

RECIPES

Rudy's Stuffed Cherry Tomatoes

Ingredients

6 hard-boiled eggs chopped

4 tablespoons minced green pepper

4 tablespoons minced ripe olives

4 tablespoons minced green onion

¼ cup mayonnaise

1 teaspoon of salt

dash of black pepper

fresh parsley

30 cherry tomatoes

Combine the eggs, green pepper, olives and onion. Blend in the mayonnaise, salt, and pepper. Add the egg mixture to the mayonnaise mixture and chill for at least one hour. Cut the tomatoes into fourths like petals, but do not cut all the way through. Use a melon ball scoop's large end and scoop one helping into the middle of the tomato. Top with tiny sprigs of parsley.

Yield: 30 stuffed tomatoes

The Mustang Lounge's Chicken Liver Spread
(make it the night before to cut down on party stress)
Ingredients
½ pound of chicken livers
1/3 cup all-purpose flour
¼ teaspoon salt
¼ teaspoon pepper
2 hard-boiled eggs
¼ medium onion
mayonnaise
sherry (the good stuff)

Salt and pepper the chicken livers and dredge in the flour. Sauté in the butter until cooked through and crisp, about 20 min. Chill thoroughly. Put the chilled chicken livers, 1 hard-boiled egg, and the onion though a food grinder or a food processor (even a blender will work but you have to keep stirring it). Add a splash of sherry and enough mayonnaise to moisten to a spreadable consistency. Chill overnight. Spread the mixture on Melba toast or crackers, and grate the yoke of the second egg over the top.

Yield: 30-40 crackers

Irish Donna's Orange Mini Muffins

Ingredients

½ cup (1 stick) butter
1 cup granulated sugar
2 eggs separated
2 cups all-purpose flour
1 teaspoon baking
    powder
2/3 cup milk
1 teaspoon lemon extract
the juice and rind zest of
    one orange

the juice and rind zest of one lemon
juice from one orange
1¼ cup water

Preheat the oven to 350°F (180°C, Gas Mark 4). Cream together the butter and sugar. Add the egg yolks and mix till lemon-colored. Sift together the flour and baking powder and add this alternately with the milk to the first mixture. Add the lemon extract. Beat the egg whites until stiff and fold in. Drop by spoonfuls into small greased muffin tins until 2/3 full. Bake for 20 minutes, or until an inserted toothpick comes out clean.

Mix the zest with the juice of the two oranges and one lemon. While the muffins are still hot, dip them first into the juice mixture then the sugar. Place on wax paper to cool.

Yield: 2-3 dozen mini muffins

Fiona's Tea Party Punch

Ingredients

2 cups boiling water
2 teaspoons tea leaves
1 cup extra-fine powdered sugar
2 cups white grape juice

4 lemons juiced
2¼ cups pineapple juice
1 quart ginger ale
vodka (optional—and to taste)
lime slices
raspberries (1 pint)
mint sprigs
(vodka if you feel the need)

Pour boiling water over tea; cover and seep for 3 minutes, and then strain. Combine the tea, sugar, and fruit juices and chill. Add the ginger ale and vodka just before serving. Served over cracked ice and garnish with raspberries, lime slices and mint. Serve in wine glasses.

Yield: 2½ cups

Irma's Easy Melon and Berry Surprise
Ingredients
1 cup mandarin oranges
1 cup white grapes
1 cups strawberries
1 cups blueberries
1 cantaloupe, halved
2 cups Grand Mariner liqueur

Marinate the grapes, oranges and berries in the Grand Mariner for 90 minutes. Hollow the cantaloupe using a melon baller. Mix the cantaloupe balls with the other marinated fruit and serve in a glass bowl with a slotted spoon to drain off the liquid, or serve in the hallowed-out cantaloupe halves. (Make a doughnut out of a paper towel or a pretty napkin and set the halves in the middle so they sit up.)

Yield: 10 ½ servings

Evie's Cheesecake
Ingredients
1¾ cup fine graham cracker crumbs
¼ cup finely chopped walnuts
½ teaspoon cinnamon
½ cup melted butter
1 pint of sliced strawberries

Preheat the oven to 350°F (180° C, Gas Mark 4). Combine all the ingredients. Save 3 tablespoons for garnish. Press the rest into the bottom of a 9-inch pie pan to form the crust.

Filling
3 eggs, well beaten
8 ounces of cream cheese, softened
1 cup granulated sugar
¼ teaspoon salt
2 teaspoons vanilla
½ teaspoon almond extract
3 cups sour cream
strawberries

Combine the eggs, cheese, sugar, salt and extracts. Beat till smooth. Blend in sour cream. Pour on top and sprinkle with reserved crumbs. Bake for 35 minutes. Chill at least 4 hours and top with fresh strawberries before serving.

Yield: 6-8 slices

"You can kill me when I no longer enjoy a cup of tea"
—Carrie Tiffany, *author*

YELLOW ROSE OF TEXAS TEA
by Leann Sweeney

MENU
Spicy Pimento Cheese on Texas Toast
Texas Tortilla Snacks (roll-ups)
Shot Glass Appetizers
Texas Brownies

INTRODUCTION
Abby Rose and her twin, Kate, don't often do anything too fancy, and Abby might spike her iced tea with a little something stronger than sugar. Abby runs Yellow Rose Investigations hoping to reunite adoptees with their birth parents. It can be a tricky and dangerous business at times. Kate, the vegetarian, makes a mean pimento cheese. In Texas, pimento cheese is one of the basic food groups, after all.

The setting for a Texas Tea is always downhome friendly and relaxed. The tablecloth with its big red checks graces a picnic table in the spring, with red or white napkins as an accompaniment. Since Texas is the Lone Star State, decorate your table with red, white and blue stars—the colors of the Texas flag.

The Tea
Cowboy's Kickback Iced Tea with Lemon
(Serve in Mason jars—if you've got them!)

RECIPES

Spicy Pimento Cheese on Texas Toast
Ingredients
10 ounces cream cheese, softened
1 tablespoon garlic powder
1 tablespoon onion powder
1 teaspoon celery seed
¾ cup mayonnaise
1 cup pickled Jalapenos, chopped
1 6-ounce jar piquillo peppers or pimentos, chopped
5 cups (about 1¼ pounds) shredded Cheddar cheese
1-2 tablespoons of your favorite hot sauce

Combine the cream cheese, garlic powder, onion powder, celery seed, and mayonnaise. Mix in the pickled jalapenos, piquillo peppers, and grated Cheddar. Add the hot sauce and combine. Taste and add more mayo and hot sauce if necessary. Chill before serving. Serve on Texas toast (which is toasted thick white bread).

Yield: approximately 1 quart

Texas Tortilla Snacks (roll-ups)
Ingredients
1 teaspoon cumin, divided
1½ teaspoon chili powder, divided
¾ pounds boneless, skinless chicken breasts
1 cup water
1 can diced tomatoes, drained
6 ounces cream cheese, softened
1 cup shredded Cheddar or Monterey Jack cheese
1 clove garlic, minced
½ teaspoon cayenne pepper
½ teaspoon garlic salt
4 tablespoons cilantro, chopped
3 scallions, white and green parts, chopped

3-4 large flour tortillas

Season the chicken breasts with salt, half of the cumin, and ¾ teaspoon of the chili powder. Add the chicken to a skillet and add about 1 cup of water. Cover and cook on med-high heat until the chicken is cooked through. Add more water if necessary. Once the chicken is cooked, cool slightly and shred with 2 forks. In a mixing bowl, combine the cream cheese, drained tomatoes, cheese, remaining spices, garlic, cilantro, and scallions. Mix together until well incorporated. Add the cooled chicken and stir together.

Lay out the tortillas and divide the mixture evenly in the center of each. Spread into a thin layer leaving the edges clean. Roll each tortilla tightly. Do not fold in the ends as you would with a burrito, but leave them free. Use a sharp knife to cut into 1" thick slices and transfer to a serving platter. (The end pieces will unroll a little so dispose of or eat the extras). Cover with plastic wrap and refrigerate until ready to serve.

Yield: 20-30 pinwheels

Shot Glass Appetizers
Ingredients
Ranch salad dressing
Celery sticks
Carrot sticks
Green olives
Cherry or grape tomatoes

Place the dressing in the bottom of a shot glass. Add a few celery and carrot sticks, and one or two skewered olives, and cherry tomatoes on a colorful toothpick.

Yield: Varies

Texas Brownies

Ingredients
2 cups all-purpose flour
2 cups granulated sugar
1 stick of butter
½ cup of shortening
1 cup water
¼ cup unsweetened cocoa
½ cup of buttermilk
2 eggs
1 teaspoon baking soda
1 teaspoon Madagascar vanilla

Frosting
1 stick (½ cup) of butter
2 tablespoons unsweetened cocoa
¼ cup milk
3½ cups unsifted confectioner's sugar
1 teaspoon Madagascar vanilla

Preheat the oven to 400°F (200°C, Gas Mark 6.) In large mixing bowl, combine the flour and the sugar. In heavy saucepan, combine butter, water and cocoa. Stir and heat to boiling. Pour the boiling mixture over the flour and sugar. Add the buttermilk, eggs, baking soda and vanilla. Mix well using a wooden spoon or high speed on an electric mixer. Pour into well-buttered 17 ½-by-11 inch jelly roll pan. Bake for 20 minutes or until the brownies test done in center.

While the brownies bake, prepare the frosting. In medium saucepan, combine butter, cocoa and milk. Heat to boiling, stirring entire time. Mix in the confectioner's sugar the until frosting is smooth. Pour warm frosting over brownies as soon as you take them out of the oven. Cool. Cut into small squares.

Yield: about 48 brownies

"Life is like a cup of tea. It's all in how you make it."
—Irish Proverb

TEA AT LAMBSPUN
by Maggie Sefton

The Menu
Chutney Cheese Finger Sandwiches
Hot Crab Canapés
Savory Scones
Butterscotch Brownies
Crème Brulee
Velvet Spice Cake

—Also on the table—
Fresh butter
Blackberry Jam

Lambspun Knitting Shop Charity Tea Menu
Hosted by, Mimi Shafer Parker,
owner of Lambspun Knitting Shop

INTRODUCTION
I wanted to host a special event which would draw in all
of Lambspun's friends, regular shoppers, and hopefully
members of the Fort Connor, Colorado community. The
new Children's Care Unit at our local Fort Collins Hospital is halfway completed. It will benefit all of the families
in our community, so that's why this charity event is dear
to my heart.

THE TABLE
I have my special Austrian white lace tablecloth and my
grandmother Susan's favorite china teacups and dessert
plates with a delicate pattern of violets. And I'm using my
mother's Royal Albert bone china Chantilly teapot. I have

to admit, the normally cluttered Lambspun knitting table never looked so pretty. Café owner Pete and I have shared preparation of the recipes, and Pete's young niece Cassie helped, too. The recipes came from a vintage cookbook I'd found years ago in a garage sale. The cover was torn off, and it was a little tattered, but the recipes were wonderful.

I sincerely hope you folks will drop by Lambspun knitting shop and enjoy our Tea Menu. We created it especially for you!

TEAS
Darjeeling—-Single estate black tea from India
Emperor's Chai—with cardamom, cinnamon & other spices
Lapsang Souchong—-Chinese smoked tea

DON'T FORGET THE FLOWERS
Abby Knight, from Kate Collins' Flower Shop Mysteries says…

The site of Maggie Sefton's Knitting Mysteries, Lambspun in Ft. Collins, Colorado, is a unique and beautifully landscaped property that attracts thousands of visitors from many states every year. This nearly 2-acre property is an oasis of flowers, trees, grass, and buildings from a simple time. The Mediterranean style buildings and courtyard were built in 1937 on a Fort Collins homestead property. The estate consists of a farmhouse and two associated outbuildings: a detached Carriage House and a small cook house and canning room building, now known as the Stone Tea House.

For a tea party here, Abby would look for flowers native to the state, including the state flower, Rocky Mountain Columbine:

Flowers

Dianthus — also known as pinks, a member of the carnation family. Choose large blossoms to compliment the smaller blossoms below.

Liatrus - try *liatris spicata,* a pink purple, or *liatris tenuifolia,* a purple pink.

Blossoms are on long spikes.

Oxeye Daisy *(leucanthemum vulgare)* a delicate white blossom.

Rocky Mountain Penstemon —or try penstemon parryi, a magenta pink. Some varieties are known as the firecracker plant. Flowers are shaped like bells.

Rocky Mountain Columbine *(aquilegia caerulea)* or Colorado Blue, a two-toned flower. Choose pale blue.

Container: Wind pretty multicolored yarn around a clay pot sprayed with adhesive.

RECIPES

Chutney Cheese Finger Sandwiches
Ingredients
12 ounces cream cheese (1 plus ½ 8-ounce size)
½ cup chutney—cut up the large pieces and use the juice
½ cup slivered blanched almonds, browned in butter
1 teaspoon mustard
½ teaspoon curry powder (more to taste)

Mix the softened cream cheese with the almonds and chutney. Add the curry powder (more to taste until the desired strength is obtained). Add the mustard. Mix all ingredients well.

Neatly trim the crusts from 6 to 8 fresh bread slices. Lightly spread each slice with the mixture. Combine two slices together into sandwiches. Cut each sandwich into four triangles. Serve.

Yield: 12-16 finger sandwiches

Hot Crab Canapés

Ingredients

1 cup fresh lump crabmeat
4 tablespoons mayonnaise
1 teaspoon tarragon vinegar
1 teaspoon lemon juice
1 tablespoon caper juice (if desired)
salt and pepper to taste
½ teaspoon dry mustard
1 tablespoon minced chives
2 tablespoons grated cheese
paprika to garnish

Combine all the ingredients except the cheese and paprika. Spread in a pie plate; sprinkle the cheese and paprika on top. Broil just to heat through. Spread on toast rounds or crackers and serve.

Yield: Approximately 12 appetizers

Savory Scones

Ingredients

1½ cups seedless green grapes
2½ cups all-purpose flour
2 tablespoons granulated sugar
1 tablespoon baking powder
¼ teaspoon salt
6 tablespoons butter
1 egg, lightly beaten
1 8-ounce carton (1 cup) of light cream
¼ cup whipping cream
1 tablespoon chopped fresh rosemary (thyme or basil)

Preheat the oven to 400°F (200°C, Gas Mark 6). Place the grapes on an ungreased baking sheet. Roast for 20 to 25 minutes or until browned and starting to burst; set aside.

In a large bowl combine the flour, sugar, baking powder and salt. Using a pastry blender, blend in butter until mixture resembles coarse crumbs. Make a well in center of flour mixture; set aside. In a medium bowl combine egg, light cream and whipping cream. Add the egg mixture all at once to flour mixture. Sprinkle with the roasted grapes and rosemary or thyme or basil as desired). Using a fork, stir just until moistened.

Turn the dough out onto a lightly floured surface. Knead the dough by folding and gently pressing it for 10-12 strokes or until it is nearly smooth. Pat the dough into a 10 x 14-inch rectangle. Cut in half lengthwise and in sixths crosswise to make 12 rectangles. Place the rectangles 2 inches apart on an ungreased baking sheet. Brush the rectangles with additional whipping cream. Bake for 13 to 15 minutes or until golden brown. Remove the scones from baking sheet. Serve warm.

Yield: 12 scones.

Butterscotch Brownies
Ingredients
1 12-ounce package butterscotch morsels
¼ cup butter
1 cup brown sugar, packed
2 eggs
½ teaspoon vanilla extract
¾ cup all-purpose flour
1 teaspoon baking powder
½ cup walnuts
Preheat the oven to 350°F (180°C, Gas Mark 4). Melt the butterscotch morsels with butter in pot over low heat. Remove from heat and add the brown sugar. Let stand 5 minutes to cool; then stir in the eggs, vanilla, flour, baking powder, salt and nuts. Bake in greased 9 x 9 x 2-inch

pan for 25 minutes. Cut while still warm.

Yield: 12 servings

Crème brûlée
Ingredients
3 cups heavy cream
6 tablespoons sugar
6 egg yolks
2 teaspoons vanilla extract
½ cup light brown sugar, packed

Preheat the oven to 300°F (150°C, Gas Mark 2). Heat the cream in a double boiler and stir in the sugar. Beat the egg yolks until light and pour the hot cream over them gradually, stirring vigorously. Stir in the vanilla and pour the mixture into a 9 x 9 x 2-inch glass baking dish. Place the dish into a larger pan containing 1 inch of hot water and place in oven. Bake for 35 minutes, or until a knife inserted into the center comes out clean. Do not over-bake; the custard will continue to cook from retained heat when it is removed from the oven. Chill thoroughly. Before serving, cover the surface with the brown sugar. Place the dish under the broiler for just a few seconds until the sugar is melted. Serve immediately, or chill again and serve cold.

Yield: 12 servings

Velvet Spice Cake
Ingredients
¾ cup butter
1½ cups granulated sugar
3 egg yolks
2 cups sifted all-purpose flour
1 teaspoon baking powder

1 teaspoon baking soda
1 teaspoon cinnamon
½ teaspoon cloves
½ teaspoon salt
7/8 cup milk (7 ounces), soured
by adding
   1 tablespoon vinegar
3 egg whites

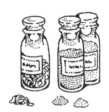

Preheat the oven to 350°F (180°C, Gas Mark 4). Beat the softened butter until fluffy. Gradually beat in the sugar, then beat in the egg yolks. The batter should be light in color and fluffy. In a separate bowl, mix together the flour, baking powder, baking soda, the spices and salt and gradually stir into the batter, adding the soured milk in between. When the batter is smooth, whip the three egg whites until stiff and gently fold them into the batter. Butter a 9-inch square pan or a loaf pan, and dust lightly with flour. Fill the pan and bake for approximately one hour. Cake comes slightly away from the pan when it is done.

Yield: 16-20 squares. If using a loaf pan, cut into 8 slices, then cut slices in half.

"You can't get a cup of tea big enough or a book long enough to suit me."
—**C.S. Lewis**, *novelist, poet, academic*

GOING COASTAL WITH OLIVIA LIMOGES TEA
by Ellery Adams

MENU
Spearmint Iced Tea
Chilled Shrimp Salad Tea Sandwiches
Chocolate Lovers' Icebox Cake
Mini Lemon Meringue Tarts
Watermelon with Seasonal Berries

INTRODUCTION
It's the height of summer. The air feels like pea soup. The beaches of North Carolina are crammed with bronzed bodies (and some sun-burned ones too), the ocean sparkles beneath the July sun, and sidewalks of Oyster Bay, the fictional setting of the Books By the Bay Mysteries, are crowded with tourists. All across town, air conditioning units are working overtime. Everyone feels hot, sticky, and tired. Locals and tourists alike would love nothing more than to sit in a cool, shady place and recharge while enjoying a delicious and refreshing mid-day treat. At The Boot Top Bistro, Oyster Bay's restaurant with the view of the lighthouse and the sailboats bobbing on their mooring lines in the harbor, refreshment is on today's menu. So come inside and prepare to be rejuvenated.

SETTING THE TABLE
The Boot Top is the area between the water lines of a ship when fully loaded or unloaded, and the restaurant was given this name as a nod to Oyster Bay's rich nautical his-

tory. To create a cool feeling on a hot, summer day, opt for a sea-colored tablecloth. The navy of a cool, dark ocean or the teal of a Caribbean pool will invoke a sense of coastal tranquility. It's too hot to light candles, so fill a hurricane vase with shells and scatter a few starfish across the table. To echo the boating theme, use nautical rope or twine to secure white or blue-and-white napkins, and to heighten the beachside feel, opt for rattan, rope, or bamboo placemats. Olivia Limoges would recommend that you keep your color palette light and simple. Let it serve as a cool backdrop for your food. And don't forget to have fun, because going coastal means leaving the hectic, busy world behind while taking deep breaths of salt-laced air and splashing through the waves as they curl onto shore. This tea is an extension of that feeling. A chance to escape with a friend for an hour or two.

Enjoy!

THE TEA
Spearmint Iced Tea (served in tall glasses and garnished with fresh sprigs of spearmint).

Spearmint tea is known for its refreshing and soothing qualities. As an iced tea, it can be served sweetened or unsweetened. This recipe is unsweetened, but if you'd like to add sugar, you can do so while the tea is steeping.

RECIPES

Spearmint Iced Tea
Ingredients
4 cups water
1 bunch fresh spearmint
4 family-size tea bags (such as Lipton Cold Brew)

In a saucepan over medium heat, bring the water to a boil. Add the mint and tea bags. Turn off the heat and allow the mint and tea to steep for 30 minutes. Remove the mint and tea bags. Discard. Pour the mixture into a container and fill with cold water until total amount of liquid equals 1 gallon. Chill for 2-4 hours. Serve over ice.

Yield: 1 gallon

Chilled Shrimp Salad Tea Sandwiches
Ingredients
1 pound cooked shrimp, peeled and de-veined
½ cup mayonnaise
¼ cup red onion, finely diced
1/3 cup chopped celery (about two stalks)
2 tablespoons lemon juice
1 tablespoon chopped fresh dill
dash celery salt
¼ teaspoon salt
¼ teaspoon pepper
8 lettuce leaves
16 slices very thin bread, crusts removed (alternating dark and light bread makes for an attractive arrangement. Try white and wheat, for example.)

Place the shrimp in a food processor and press pulse until finely minced. Transfer the shrimp to a bowl and add the onion, celery, lemon juice, dill, and seasonings. Mix well. Chill the shrimp salad for one hour. When ready to serve, layer half the slices of bread with lettuce. Spread the shrimp salad over the lettuce and top with the remaining bread. Cut into triangles. Serve immediately.

Yield: 8 servings (32 fingers sandwiches)

Chocolate Lovers' Icebox Cake
Ingredients
2 cups cold heavy cream
12 ounces mascarpone cheese
½ cup granulated sugar
2 tablespoons unsweetened cocoa powder
1 teaspoon pure vanilla extract
1 package (9 ounces) chocolate wafer cookies*
Chocolate shavings for garnish (dark or semisweet)

In a large bowl, blend the heavy cream, mascarpone cheese, sugar, cocoa powder, and vanilla with an electric mixer. Continue mixing until stiff peaks form. Line an 8 ½ -x- 4 ½-inch loaf pan with parchment paper. Layer the mascarpone mixture and half of the package of chocolate wafer cookies in the prepared pan. Begin and end with the mascarpone mixture. (You'll end up with 3 layers of cake and 2 layers of cookies). Refrigerate for at least 12 hours. To remove from the pan, first run a knife around outside of cake. Cut in slices and garnish with chocolate curls.

*To give this cake a minty flavor, simply replace the chocolate wafer cookies with mint chocolate wafers

Yield: 10 servings

Mini Lemon Meringue Tarts
Crust
1¼ cups graham cracker crumbs
3 tablespoons packed brown sugar
5 tablespoons unsalted butter, melted

Filling
3 eggs, separated
½ cup granulated sugar

2 tablespoons cornstarch
1 cup water
1 cup all-purpose flour
6 tablespoons freshly squeezed lemon juice
1 tablespoon freshly grated lemon zest
1 tablespoon butter
½ cup granulated sugar
½ teaspoon cream of tartar

Preheat oven to 350°F (180°C, Gas Mark 4). Place a metal mixing bowl and beater attachments in the freezer (this will help in making your meringue later on). Mix the graham cracker crumbs, brown sugar, and butter. Press 2 heaping tablespoons of the mixture into the bottom of each muffin tin. Press down with a shot glass or your fingers. Bake for 10 minutes. For the filling: Whisk the sugar, cornstarch, and flour in saucepan. Add in the water, lemon juice, and lemon zest and bring to a boil over medium heat, stirring constantly. Reduce the heat to a simmer. Add the egg yolks and butter, whisking the mixture until it is thick and smooth. Spoon the hot lemon filling into the crusts. Remove the metal bowl and beater attachments from the freezer. Beat the egg whites, sugar, and cream of tartar in the chilled bowl with electric mixer until the meringue forms stiff peaks. Spread about 1 inch of the meringue onto each pie and form peaks with a rubber spatula. Bake until the meringue is golden brown. About 10 minutes.) Let cool completely before serving.

Yield: 6 servings

Watermelon with Seasonal Berries
Ingredients
  cups cubed watermelon
  ounces fresh blueberries
  ounces fresh blackberries

3 tablespoons water
3 tablespoons granulated sugar
1 teaspoon grated lemon zest
1 tablespoon fresh mint leaves, finely chopped

In a saucepan over medium heat, bring the water and sugar to a boil. Remove from the heat and let cool. Combine the fruit, lemon zest, and mint in large bowl. Pour the sugar syrup on top of the fruit mixture. Gently toss until the fruit is evenly coated. Serve in individual bowls with a dollop of whipped cream. A chilled fork would add a finishing note of luxurious refreshment to your "going coastal" tea.

Yield: 6 servings

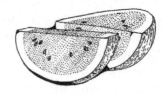

"I shouldn't think even millionaires could eat anything nicer than new bread and real butter and honey for tea."
—**Dodie Smith**, *English novelist and playwright*

TEDDY BEAR'S TEA
by Mary Jane Maffini

MENU
Raspberry tea
Peanut butter and honey triangles
Red ants on logs
Chocolate almond bark
Oatmeal blueberry squares
Meringue kisses

INTRODUCTION
My name is Charlotte Adams. I am a busy professional organizer and, yes, single still at thirtysomething. I adore my oldest friend, Sally, and I'm crazy about Sally's four children. I love spending time with them and giving their mom a break. Being with little kids gives me a whole new view of the world. Dallas, Savannah, Madison and baby Shenandoah love teddy bears. I'd never thought much about them, but they've been hinting about a party for their bears. There's a terrific new tea shop that offers afternoon tea in our town of Woodbridge, New York (on the Hudson). It's given me an idea. Now I'm very excited about setting up a Teddy Bears' Tea for my little friends and their little bears. The children are helping me plan it. We're learning as we go.

They've discovered that bears eat what they can find in the woods: honey, nuts, flowers, fruit, berries, and, um, insects. I've picked some recipes that are simple enough for children to make under supervision and cover these food groups. I should mention that the oatmeal blueberry square recipe would be a better cooking challenge for older children and not toddlers.

With their help making these easy recipes, my special tea party ensures that the bears have all their favorites, plus a few special treats for any little girls who might be invited. We all know that in an enchanted wood, in addition to fruit, berries etc., bears might also find chocolate and meringues.

SETTING THE TABLE

I found a vintage blue-and-white tablecloth with little hearts on it. It will go nicely with the pretty (and unbreakable) small white dishes and cups we've selected. We weren't entirely sure that bears mightn't be a bit unused to tea parties. We know they like flowers. We were going to select daisies to decorate the table, but we decided on nasturtiums. We love the bright yellow and orange flowers and they pop next to the blue and white tablecloth, but also the bears can eat them and so can we. Because you just never know.

TEA

Raspberry tea is a lovely way to capture the juicy, fruitiness of this delicious berry. Bears and children enjoy finding and picking this summer treat.

RECIPES

Peanut Butter and Honey Triangles
Ingredients
4 slices white or wheat toast
4 teaspoons of softened unsalted butter
4 tablespoons smooth peanut butter
4 tablespoons favorite honey (Clover honey is especially good. Ask any bear!)

Butter the toast. Spread 1 tablespoon of peanut butter on

each piece of buttered toast. Spread a tablespoon of honey on top of the peanut butter on each slice. Cut the toast into triangles. You can always cut off the crusts, but they help to keep the honey on!

Yield: 8 servings of two triangles each

Red Ants on Logs
All bears love ants, so these are a big hit with teddy bears and their human friends.
Ingredients
4 medium celery stalks
6 tablespoons of cream cheese, softened
¼ cup of sweetened dried cranberries

Fill the hollows of celery stalks with the cream cheese. Level them off. Dot the cream cheese in each stalk with dried cranberries. Cut each stalk in half. If cream cheese is not to your taste, you can also do these fun snacks with peanut butter and raisins if that suits.

Yield: 8 logs and many red ants

Chocolate Almond Bark
Ingredients
1 8-ounce package semi-sweet chocolate pieces or chips
1 cup slivered almonds, toasted
½ cup raisins or sweetened dried cranberries (craisins)

Microwave the chocolate in a small microwaveable bowl on medium for 1 to 2 minutes or until the chocolate is almost melted. Stir until completely melted. Stir in the nuts and then the raisins or cranberries while it's still warm. Spread onto parchment paper (or waxed paper) covered baking sheet. Refrigerate for 30 minutes or until firm. Break into pieces.

Yield: Enough for 10 hungry bears

Meringue Kisses
Ingredients
4 egg whites (from extra-large eggs, at room temperature)
1/8 teaspoon cream of tartar
1 teaspoon good quality vanilla
½ teaspoon almond extract (optional)
1 cup minus 1 tablespoon granulated sugar

Preheat oven to 225°F (110°C, Gas Mark 1/4). Beat the egg whites with the cream of tartar until soft peaks form. Add the vanilla and almond (if using). Very slowly add the sugar tablespoon by tablespoon, beating well after every addition, until stiff peaks form. Line two baking sheets with parchment paper. Use a tablespoon to dab on the meringue mixture—a heaping tablespoon per meringue. Swirl the meringue with the back of a spoon, twisting the top of each cookie to make a little point (for kisses). Meringue is lots of fun and if you have a problem with one swirl, you can just do it again.

Bake for 18 to 20 minutes. Don't let the kisses brown at the edges. If your oven runs hot, reduce temperature. After twenty minutes (if they haven't begun to brown) turn off heat and allow them to 'dry' for one to two hours before serving.

Yield: 3 dozen small meringue kisses

Oatmeal Blueberry Squares
Ingredients
1½ cups large flaked oatmeal (not instant)
1 cup unbleached white flour
1 cup light brown sugar, packed
1/8 teaspoon salt
1½ teaspoons baking powder

1 cup butter, melted
2 cups blueberries
2 tablespoons cornstarch
½ cup granulated sugar
1 tablespoon lemon juice
1 teaspoon lemon zest
¼ cup water

Preheat the oven to 350°F (180°C, Gas Mark 4). Combine the oatmeal, flour, brown sugar, salt, and baking powder. Spread half this mixture on a greased nine-inch square cake pan and set aside. Combine the blueberries, cornstarch, white sugar, lemon juice, zest, and water in a saucepan. Cook on medium heat until the mixture is nice and thick. Cool and spread over the oatmeal mixture in cake pan. Spread the remaining oatmeal mixture on top and smooth. Bake 40 to 45 minutes or until golden brown.

Yield: 16 large squares

"I got nasty habits; I take tea at three."
—**Mick Jagger**, *lead singer, The Rolling Stones*

A MAD TEA PARTY
by Leann Sweeney

MENU

Oh, My, It's Green Tea
Crazy Scones
We're All Mad Cuke Sandwiches
Blueberry Magic Mini Muffins
Queen of Hearts Cookies

INTRODUCTION

Nothing is as it should be when it comes to a Mad Tea Party. Feel free to make your book club or garden club members or any others guests be as surprised as possible. They should experience what it is like to "go down the rabbit hole" when they visit you for this very special occasion.

SETTING THE TABLE—And Make This An Experience!

A sign on the front door can be made with a strip of balsa wood. Using a thick black or red marker print "You're Late" and hang it prominently and maybe even a little crooked. The china is mismatched, the placemats are all different, and in the center of the table is a sign easily made with markers or paint reading, "We're All Mad Here." Buy a deck of pinochle cards—the large font kind. They are almost all face cards. Cut off the corners on about half of the kings and queens. The sharp edge can be placed into your muffin tops as decoration.

If you don't have heart-shaped cookie cutters, they can be found at the dollar store or discount store at low cost. Use these for your cookies.

DON'T FORGET THE FLOWERS
Abby Knight, from Kate Collins' Flower Shop Mysteries says....

"I would have fun with this arrangement using a variety of unusual plants she'd have shipped in from Hawaii, just the sort of *mad* arrangement one might find in Alice's Wonderland. Naturally, she'd use the King, Queen, and Jack of hearts from a deck of cards on long clear plastic spikes, as well as plastic toadstools with a red cap and white polka dots as accents."

Flowers
Yellow shrimp plant
Orange Bird of paradise
Red Lobster claw
White Ladies' slipper
Red bottlebrush

Container
A brightly colored watering can (to water those mushrooms) or a straw basket with a handle. A deep straw hat would be fun, too.

RECIPES

Crazy Scones
Ingredients
1¾ cups (about 8 ounces) all-purpose flour
¼ cup granulated sugar
2 teaspoons baking powder
½ teaspoon salt
4 tablespoons (2 ounces) cold butter, cut into pieces
1/3 cup raisins, or other dried fruit
½ cup milk
1 large egg
2 tablespoons rainbow Jimmies

Preheat the oven to 425°F (220°C, Gas Mark 7). Sift together flour, sugar, baking powder and salt into large bowl. Using your fingertips or a pastry blender, rub or cut the butter into the flour mixture to form coarse crumbs. Add the raisins or other fruit. Whisk together the milk and egg. Make a well in the flour mixture; pour in the milk mixture. Using a fork, stir just until a soft, moist dough is formed. Turn the dough out onto a lightly floured surface; gently knead 1 or 2 times to incorporate loose pieces of dough. (Do not over-knead.) Pat the dough to 1½-inch thickness. Using well-floured 2½-inch diameter biscuit cutter or the top of a glass, cut out about 6 rounds. Place the rounds on a lightly-buttered baking sheet. Sprinkle with the Jimmies. Bake 14 to 17 minutes or until golden brown, rotating the pan halfway through baking for more even browning. Serve warm with butter, jam, clotted or Devonshire cream.

Yield: 6 scones

We're All Mad Cuke Sandwiches
Ingredients
½ of an 8-ounce package of cream cheese, softened
3 tablespoons finely chopped cucumber
3 ounces cold smoked salmon, thinly sliced
1 teaspoon trimmed, minced watercress
½ teaspoon lemon juice
1/8 teaspoon ground red pepper
12 bread slices
3 tablespoons butter, softened

Process the cream cheese in a food processor until smooth, stopping to scrape down the sides. Add the finely chopped cucumber and next 4 ingredients; process until well blended. Carefully spread the cut outer edges of sandwiches with butter. Spread the cucumber-salmon mixture over 6 slices. Top with the remaining bread and trim the crusts. Cut into triangles.

Yield: 24 triangular sandwiches (or 6 full-sized sandwiches)

Blueberry Magic Mini Muffins
Ingredients
1 cup all-purpose flour
¾ cup granulated sugar
1½ teaspoons baking powder
½ teaspoon salt
¾ cup blueberries (frozen, thawed are okay-but drain well)
1 egg
½ cup milk
⅛ cup canola oil
1½ teaspoons vanilla extract

Preheat the oven to 375°F (190°C, Gas Mark 5). Mix the dry ingredients in a bowl and set aside. In another bowl, whisk the wet ingredients. Add the milk mixture to the flour mixture and use a spatula to very gently fold them together for about 5 or 6 strokes. There will be lumps; do not over-mix. Spoon the batter into a greased mini muffin tin and bake for 10 to 12 minutes, or until the tops are golden brown.

Yield: 16 mini muffins

Queen of Hearts Cookies
Ingredients
2 sticks (1 cup) of butter, softened
1 cup confectioner's sugar, divided

2 teaspoons almond extract
2¼ cups all-purpose flour
¾ cup finely ground almonds
¼ teaspoon salt
½ cup milk
½ cup seedless jam of your choice

Cream together the butter and ¾ cup of the confectioner's sugar. Beat in the almond extract. In another bowl, combine the flour, almonds, and salt. Add milk and then flour mixture to the creamed butter in three batches, alternating wet and dry ingredients. Mix thoroughly at medium speed between additions. Gently knead the dough on a floured surface to form a disk. Cover with plastic and chill for at least 3 hours.

To bake, preheat the oven to 350°F (180°C, Gas Mark 4). Sift the remaining ¼ cup confectioner's sugar into a small bowl and set aside. Cut the dough in half and return one piece to refrigerator. Roll out the dough on a surface dusted with confectioner's sugar to 1/8-inch thickness. Cut out with a small heart-shaped cookie cutter about 1½ inches wide and transfer to an ungreased baking sheet. Bake for 18 to 20 minutes, or until the edges are golden brown. Transfer the cookies to wire racks. Re-roll the scraps and the remaining dough and continue cutting and baking. While the cookies are still hot, spread the bottoms of half the cookies with the jam. Place an uncoated cookie over the jelly, bottom-to-bottom and press together to sandwich the filling. Let the cookies cool and then dip each in confectioner's sugar to coat, shaking off the excess sugar. Cool on racks before storing.

Yield: approximately 40 small cookies

"His guests found it fun to watch him make tea—mixing careful spoonfuls from different caddies."
—**James Hilton**, *Good-Bye, Mr. Chips*

A SHABBY CHIC TEA
by Lorraine Bartlett

MENU
Raisin Scones
Almond Shortbread
Old-Fashioned Date Bars
Chicken Waldorf Salad Sandwiches
Ham and Cheese with Chutney Sandwiches

INTRODUCTION
Kathy Grant, here. I'm holding a special tea for my best friends, Tori Cannon, Anissa Jackson, and Noreen Darby. I'm in the process of rehabbing an old house to open a bed and breakfast and I couldn't have even started the process without the loving support of my BFFs. My friends will (unknowingly) act as Guinea pigs for these recipes which I hope to one day serve my paying guests. (Somehow, I don't think they'll mind.)

SETTING THE TABLE
Tori's grandmother was a bit of a packrat. After she passed away, Anissa and I helped Tori empty out her grandparents' house of her Grandma's "treasures." Among them were an enormous assortment of mix-and-match dishes, silverware, and bone china cups and saucers that the old lady had collected from yard and garage sales over the years. As a thank you, Tori and her grandfather offered me first pick. It's with these dishes that I intend to set my table.

Among the treasures were old stained embroidered linens and hand-crocheted doilies. Soaking them in Oxiclean, and leaving the linens to dry in the sun on grass (more oxygen!) helped to safely bleach them back to their former glory. Anyone would be proud to show off these vintage pieces of handiwork.

THE TEA
Orange Pekoe

DON'T FORGET THE FLOWERS
Abby Knight, from Kate Collins' Flower Shop Mysteries says....
Dried flower arrangements can have an impact or a subtlety equal to that of fresh blooms. And you don't have to worry about them wilting before your party guests arrive. As a rule, dried flowers work better en masse, such as dozens of tightly packed rose buds. Also, since water is not used in these arrangements, many different types of vases can be used, such as a low basket or even an umbrella stand.
For the shabby chic tea, Abby has selected the following:

Flowers
Dried roses (peach)
Poppy seed heads (vanilla colored)
Dried blue lavender
Hydrangea (green)
Curly willow (white)

Container: 5″ square glass vase filled with pebbles, seashells, stones.

RECIPES
Raisin Scones
Ingredients
2 cups all-purpose flour
4 teaspoons baking powder
½ teaspoon salt
1/3 cup sugar
4 tablespoons butter
2 tablespoons shortening
¾ cup cream or half-and-half
1 egg
½ cup raisins (can use dried currants, cranberries, or chocolate chips)

Preheat the oven to 375°F (190°C, Gas Mark 5). In a large mixing bowl, combine the flour, baking powder, salt, and sugar. Mix well. Cut in the butter and shortening. In a separate bowl, combine the cream with the beaten egg, then add to the dry ingredients. Stir in the raisins (or other fruit/chips). Turn the dough out onto a floured surface. Roll out the dough and cut it into biscuit size rounds. Bake for 15 minutes or until brown. Serve warm with butter, clotted or Devonshire cream, and/or jam.

Yield: 10-12 scones

Almond Shortbread
Ingredients
1 cup all-purpose flour
½ cup confectioner's sugar
¼ cup cornstarch
½ cup (1 stick) butter, softened
¼ teaspoon vanilla extract
¼ teaspoon almond extract
½ cup almonds, toasted and lightly crushed

Preheat the oven to 375°F (180°C, Gas Mark 4). In a food processor, combine the flour, sugar, and cornstarch. With on-off bursts, add the butter, vanilla and almond extracts, and almonds until the mixture just forms a ball. (It can be done without a food processor—it just takes a bit more work.) Pat the dough into an ungreased 8-inch round pan and smooth the top. Prick the dough all over with a fork. With a knife, score into 8 wedges.

Yield: 8 wedges

Old-Fashioned Date Bars
Ingredients
1 cup packed brown sugar
½ cup butter
¼ cup shortening
1¾ cups all-purpose flour
½ teaspoon salt
½ teaspoon baking soda
1½ cups quick-cook oats

Date Filling
1-pound (16 ounces) dates, cut up (about 3 cups)
1½ cups water
¼ cup granulated sugar

Mix the dates, water, and sugar in a saucepan and cook over low heat, stirring consistently, until thickened. (About ten minutes.)

Preheat the oven to 400°F (200°C, Gas Mark 6). Mix the brown sugar, butter, and shortening. Stir in the remaining ingredients. Press half of the crumbly mixture in a 13 x 9 x 2-inch baking pan. Spread with the filling. Top with the remaining crumbly mixture and press down lightly. Bake until a light brown, about 25 to 30 minutes. Cut into bars (2 x 1 inch) while warm.

Yield: 4 dozen bars

Chicken Waldorf Salad Sandwiches
Ingredients
3 cups cooked chicken, cut up small
¾ cup coarsely chopped walnuts
¾ cup diced apple (pick your favorite)
¼ cup celery, minced
½ cup raisins (or halved grapes)
2 scallions, minced
salt and pepper to taste

Dressing
1 cup mayonnaise (olive oil mayo has a lot less calories!)
½ cup sour cream
¼ cup cider vinegar
1 tablespoon honey
5 slices of your favorite bread
butter, room temperature

Place the salad ingredients in a large bowl and toss to combine. In a smaller bowl, whisk the dressing ingredients. Pour over the chicken mixture and mix well. Chill for an hour or more. Spread the bread with a thin coating of butter. Spread 2-3 tablespoons of salad on each of 3 slices of bread. Trim the crusts and cut into triangles.

Yield: 12 triangle finger sandwiches

Ham and Cheese with Chutney Sandwiches
Ingredients
slices bread
butter, room temperature
Black Forest ham sliced slightly thick

4 slices Swiss cheese
mango or other fruit chutney (I like peach or rhubarb)

Spread the butter on all slices of bread. Lay the ham and cheese on one side of four slices of bread. Spread some chutney on the other slices. Put the slices of bread together and press down lightly. Cut off the crusts and cut the sandwich into four triangles. Cover with a damp tea towel for up to an hour before serving.

Yield: 16 finger sandwiches

"Afternoon tea should be provided, fresh supplies, with thin bread-and-butter, fancy pastries, cakes, etc., being brought in as other guests arrive."
—**Isabella Beeton**, Mrs Beeton's Book of Household Management

CAPE BRETON ENGAGEMENT TEA
by Mary Jane Maffini

MENU
Red Rose Orange Pekoe Tea
Open-faced Smoked Salmon and Cream Cheese on Pumpernickel Canapés
Egg Salad Sweetheart Sandwiches
Traditional Scottish Oatcakes
Shortbread with Chopped Dark Chocolate
Famous Butter Tarts

INTRODUCTION
Greetings! I am Alvin Ferguson, indispensable and modest office assistant to Camilla MacPhee, the well-known victims' advocate and defense lawyer, when she isn't sleuthing irritably around the capital of Canada, Ottawa. Mostly I assist her in her work, but I often find myself drawn into the family dramas of which the MacPhees have many. Like Camilla and her older sisters Alexa, Donalda and Edwina, I am also from beautiful Cape Breton (where our friend, Lorraine Bartlett, spent her honeymoon), so I understand their family ways. The sisters sometimes despair of Camilla. I get that. She is totally undomesticated. Stubborn too.

They are very keen to have her settle down again. Camilla, if you don't know, was widowed at the age of thirty. That partly explains the chip on her shoulder, but face it, that was fifteen years ago. But for the past five of those years, she has had a happy—and relatively calm—romantic relationship with Sergeant Ray Deveau. Ray is generally considered to be a saint and, in fact, left his job as a detective on the Cape Breton Regional Police Force to join Camilla in Ottawa. Camilla's family would very much like to see them married. What can I say? We're all getting the message that a wedding may actually happen. Just little hints here and there. Camilla and Ray are the type to simply elope, but they won't be getting away with that.

Alexa, Donalda and Edwina are excellent cooks and remember the era when teas were held with style, taste and matching dishes. Therefore, the MacPhee sisters are proud to offer this version of an afternoon tea for Camilla using the recipes they grew up with on Cape Breton Island. The recipes reflect their Scottish heritage, and oatcakes, shortbread, and butter tarts are among the best traditions.

The sisters would love this party to be an 'engagement' tea for Camilla and the long-suffering Detective Sergeant Ray Deveau. In fact, you may notice several diamond and heart-shaped delicacies as part of the theme but Camilla's sisters may have to settle for just having her behave for the event.

Some might say Camilla's sisters are just the tiniest bit competitive and, um, bossy. So what if they are? We can still have fun.

SETTING THE TABLE AND THE SCENE

Each of the sisters will contribute to the table setting. I would love to have witnessed the behind-the-scenes battles to see who does what. The tea will be held at Edwina's spacious and well-appointed home. Donalda (having lost out of being hostess) is providing her best tablecloth. She loves nothing more than a perfectly pressed white linen tablecloth, no creases, not one. I am not sure how that's achieved. Donalda's Cape Breton tartan cloth napkins will pop against that white. The white will be offset by Edwina's Minton china with its subtle pale green flower pattern. Edwina has consoled herself by polishing up Great-Grandmother MacPhee's antique silver tea service, while Alexa has produced her favorite tiered servers and cake plates for showing canapés and sweets at their best. Different heights will add visual interest, she says. Edwina has again upped the ante by producing an ornate, antique silver candelabra with green candles to complement the tartan.

My job is to trick Camilla into arriving. And, since I'm in the mood for toe-tapping fun, I've arranged for an East Coast fiddler to play some traditional Scottish and Acadian melodies. I tried for a piper, but no luck. I haven't mentioned any of this because according to the sisters, it's generally better to ask for forgiveness than permission.

The only thing missing: fireworks, although there may be some.

THE TEA

The MacPhee girls grew up on steeped orange pekoe tea by Red Rose. The water should be on the 'rolling boil.' The tea will be steeped (after the pot is warmed and that water discarded), but instead of the traditional four minute steeping, they believe in seven. It will definitely be bracing, like the sisters themselves. The tea bags or ball with loose tea should be removed after that. Red Rose Tea has been an iconic Canadian brand for over a hundred years. The Red Rose Tea advertising campaign was famous for its slogan: *Only in Canada you say? Pity...*

(Just so you know, Red Rose tea is available in the USA and is made from a different blend of black pekoe. But do come to Canada to visit to have the real thing.)

DON'T FORGET THE FLOWERS
Abby Knight, from Kate Collins' Flower Shop Mysteries says....

"I see a romantic, candlelit evening, a bottle of champagne chilling in an ice bucket, and a centerpiece in the middle filled with the most romantic flowers of all."

Flowers
White tea roses
White gardenias
White calla lilies
Maidenhair fern

Container
A tall crystal vase.

Interesting fact: Despite what their name suggests, calla lilies are not true lilies or even a calla. The flower belongs to the genus Zantedeschia and is a member of the Araceae family, along with the caladium and philodendron. It is also known as the pig lily, trumpet lily and arum lily. Why is it called a lily? Because the Swedish botanist Carolus Linnaeus made a mistake when he was naming the species. Later, the German botanist Karl Koch corrected the error and established the genus Zantedeschia, but the name stuck. Calla lilies are commonly white, but they also come in a variety of colors, including yellow, pink, green, purple, orange and black. The colored varieties are called mini calla lilies.

RECIPES

**Smoked Salmon, Cream Cheese and Dill
on Pumpernickel (Canapés)**
Ingredients
8 2-inch squares of pumpernickel bread
1 ounce (two tablespoons) cream cheese, room temperature
2 ounces smoked salmon, cut into pieces, just slightly smaller than the pumpernickel
8 tiny sprigs of fresh dill

Arrange the pumpernickel squares on a board or other surface. Spread each with 1 teaspoon of cream cheese. Arrange small pieces of smoked salmon on top of the cheese. Top with a small sprig of fresh dill. Display on a pretty plate.

Yield: 8 canapés

Best Ever Egg Salad Sandwich Hearts
Ingredients
4 extra-large eggs
¼ cup good quality mayonnaise (add more if you
    like a creamier sandwich)
½ teaspoon Dijon mustard
2 tablespoons cup finely chopped fresh chives
salt and pepper to taste (Edwina uses ½ teaspoon salt and
¼ teaspoon pepper)
8 slices day-old whole wheat bread, rolled slightly with a rolling pin
/8 cup butter, at room temperature. Make sure it's soft enough to spread.

Place the eggs in a saucepan and cover with cold water. Bring to a boil and cook on the boil for 20 minutes. Remove the pan from the heat; drain and cool rapidly in cold water. When cold, shell the eggs and chop. (We use a potato masher to get the right consistency.) Blend in the mayonnaise and mustard, salt and pepper, and chives. Lay out the eight slices of bread. Butter all eight slices. Spread the egg mixture on four slices of bread. Top with remaining four slices. Press down. Using a small heart-shaped cookie cutter, cut through sandwiches to make small hearts. If you prefer (or don't have the heart-shaped cutter), trim crusts and cut into finger sandwiches, one-half inch wide each. Arrange on a plate.

Yield: 16 small heart-shaped sandwiches

Traditional Scottish Oatcakes
Ingredients
2½ cups oatmeal (not instant and not steel-cut)
1 cup brown sugar, packed
1 cup unbleached white flour
1 teaspoon baking soda
¾ teaspoon salt
1 cup butter or shortening, softened
1 teaspoon vanilla
1 large egg, beaten

Combine the dry ingredients and cut in the shortening o butter. Add the vanilla and egg. Chill the dough for a least 30 minutes.

Preheat the oven to 350°F (180°C, Gas Mark 4). Rol out the dough to about ¼ inch thickness and cut into di amond shapes with a cookie cutter. Bake for 10 minute or until golden brown.

Yield: 2 dozen oatcakes

Famous Butter Tarts
Tart shells
2 cups all-purpose flour
1 cup butter
4 tablespoons confectioner's sugar

Preheat the oven to 425°F (220°C, Gas Mark 7). Cut the butter into the flour. Add the sugar and knead until well-blended. You can use a food processor, but do not over blend. Press small amounts of dough into small muffin tins. Bake for about 8 minutes. They shouldn't brown. Cool.

Filling
2 cups boiling water
½ cup raisins
¼ cup butter, softened
1 cup brown sugar, packed
1 egg, beaten
1 tablespoon lemon juice

Preheat the oven to at 375°F (190°C, Gas Mark 5). Pour the boiling water over the raisins and let stand for ten minutes. Drain. Cream the butter. Gradually add the sugar and mix well. Add the beaten egg a little at a time, blending well after each addition. Stir in the drained raisins and the lemon juice. Fill the cooled pastry shells with a teaspoon of the mixture. Bake for 15 to 20 minutes until the pastry is golden and filling is set.

Yield: 24 small tarts

Shortbread with Chopped Dark Chocolate
Ingredients
2 cups all-purpose flour
½ cup confectioner's sugar

1 cup unsalted butter, cut into cubes
2 ounces of dark chocolate, coarsely chopped (although you could substitute milk chocolate or semi-sweet chocolate chips)

Preheat the oven to 300°F (150°C, Gas Mark 2). Mix the flour and sugar together in a bowl. Cut in the butter or mix in with a food processor. Work in the chocolate pieces. (Do not process chocolate in the food processor.) Wrap the dough in wax paper (or cloth or even plastic wrap) and cool in the refrigerator for at least 15 minutes. Roll the dough out on a floured surface to about 1/3 inch thick. Cut into rectangles with a knife or use cookie cutters to make fancy shapes, such as circles to represent eternity or moon shapes for a honeymoon. (You can cut them a bit thicker, but they may need to bake a bit longer.) Bake at on the middle rack for 18 to 20 minutes. They shouldn't brown, that will change the taste.

Yield: 3 dozen shortbread

"There are those who love to get dirty and fix things. They drink coffee at dawn, beer after work. And those who stay clean, just appreciate things. At breakfast they have milk and juice at night. There are those who do both, they drink tea."
—**Gary Snyder**, *American Poet*

TEATIME AT SASSY SALLY'S
BED AND BREAKFAST
by Lorraine Bartlett

THE MENU
Honey Apple Salad
Apple-Cinnamon Scones
Apple Butter
Apple-Cheese Tea Sandwiches
Applesauce Cake
Baked Apple

INTRODUCTION
Katie Bonner spent many years dreaming about opening the English Ivy Inn. It would be a magical place for brides and grooms to say, "I do," for honeymooning couples, and for couples to spend many a romantic anniversary weekend. It would be a place of rest and beauty and her many guests would return again and again to her beautifully restored Victorian mansion on the edge of Victoria Square.

Sadly, her husband banished those dreams when instead he invested their money in Artisans Alley, an arts-and-crafts arcade at the other end of Victoria Square. It was a going concern quickly going downhill. After both her husband and its manager died, Katie had to step in to save her investment. And then the mansion was sold—not once but twice before she could recover financially.

The English Ivy Inn was never to be. But Katie still

fantasizes about it. How she would have beautifully re-stored it, and played hostess at the many afternoon teas for guests. Instead, she has shared her ideas with the current owners of the home she once coveted. It's now called Sassy Sally's.

Victoria Square is a quaint business district in the small town of McKinlay Mill, which is surrounded by apple orchards. What better fruit could Katie use as the basis for one of her afternoon teas?

RECIPES

Honey Apple Salad
Ingredients
3½ cups diced red apples
2 tablespoons lemon juice
2 cups green grapes
1 cup chopped celery
½ cup chopped dates
½ cup mayonnaise
¼ cup honey
2 tablespoons sour cream
¼ teaspoon salt
½ cup chopped walnuts (optional)

In a large bowl, toss the apples with the lemon juice. Add the grapes, celery, and dates. In a small bowl, whisk the mayonnaise, honey, sour cream, and salt. Pour the mixture over the fruit and toss to coat. Stir in the walnuts. Serve immediately or chill before serving.

Yield: 6-8 servings

Apple-Cinnamon Scones

Ingredients

2 cups all-purpose flour
¼ cup granulated sugar
2 teaspoons baking powder
½ teaspoon baking soda
½ teaspoon salt
¼ cup butter, chilled
1 apple, peeled, cored and grated
½ cup milk
2 tablespoons milk
2 tablespoons granulated sugar
½ teaspoon ground cinnamon

Preheat the oven to 425°F (220°C, Gas Mark 7). Combine the flour, sugar, baking powder, soda, and salt into a large bowl. Cut in the butter until crumbly. Add the grated apple and milk. Stir to form a soft dough. Turn the dough out onto a lightly floured surface. Knead gently 8 to 10 times. Pat into two 6-inch circles. Place on a greased baking sheet. Brush tops with milk and sprinkle with sugar and cinnamon. Score each into 6 pie-shaped wedges. Bake for 15 minutes or until golden brown and risen. Serve warm with butter, apple butter, clotted cream, or whipped cream.

Yield: 12 servings

Apple Butter

Ingredients

½ pounds apples, peeled, cored, and finely chopped
2 cups granulated sugar
2 teaspoons ground cinnamon
¼ teaspoon ground cloves
¼ teaspoon salt

Place the apples in a slow cooker. In a medium bowl, mix the sugar, cinnamon, cloves and salt. Pour the mixture over the apples in the slow cooker and mix well. Cover and cook on high 1 hour. Reduce the heat to low and cook 9 to 11 hours, stirring occasionally, until the mixture is thickened and dark brown. Uncover and continue cooking on low for another hour. Stir with a whisk, if desired, to increase smoothness. Remove to sterilized jars, cool, and cap.

Yield: 4 pints

Apple-Cheese Tea Sandwiches

Ingredients

8 slices (commercial) cinnamon raisin bread
1 8-ounce package of cream cheese, softened
    or ¼ cup softened butter
4 slices Havarti or Cheddar cheese
1 large Granny Smith apple, cored and thinly sliced

Spread a thin layer of cream cheese (or softened butter on 4 slices of bread. Top the cream cheese (or butter) with a slice of Havarti cheese, then a thin layer of apple slices. Place the remaining slices of bread on top to form 4 sandwiches. Trim the crusts. Using 2 diagonal cuts, divide each sandwich into 4 triangles.

Yield: 16 triangle finger sandwiches

Applesauce Cake

Ingredients

1½ cups unsweetened applesauce
1 egg
1 cup granulated sugar
2 tablespoons butter
1 teaspoon vanilla extract

2 cups all-purpose flour
2 teaspoons baking soda
½ teaspoon ground cinnamon
¼ teaspoon ground cloves
¼ teaspoon ground nutmeg
1 cup raisins
1 cup chopped walnuts

Preheat the oven to 350°F (180°C, Gas Mark 4). In a mixing bowl, combine the first five ingredients. In another bowl, combine the flour, baking soda, and spices. Mix the wet and dry ingredients until smooth. Pour into two greased 8-inch x 4-inch x 2-inch loaf pans. Bake for 45 to 55 minutes or until a toothpick inserted near the center comes out clean. Cool for 10 minutes before removing the cakes from the pans to wire racks.

Yield: 12-16 servings

Baked Apples
4 tart apples (such as Granny Smith or Cortland)
4 teaspoons chopped walnuts or pecans
4 tablespoons brown sugar, packed
4 teaspoons raisins
4 tablespoons butter
1 teaspoon cinnamon

Preheat oven to 375°F (190°C, Gas Mark 5). Butter a baking dish. Cut the top off each apple. Core and seed each apple, but don't cut through the bottom. Mix the nuts, brown sugar, and raisins together. Fill the apples with the mix and dot them with butter. Bake until the apples are soft but not mushy. (About 25 minutes.) Serve hot or warm with vanilla ice cream or whipped cream

Yield: 4 servings

"At Christmas, tea is compulsory. Relatives are optional."
—**Robert Godden**, *author*

CHRISTMAS TEA AT STORYTON HALL
by Ellery Adams

MENU
Black Tea with Orange Peel
Cranberry Chicken Salad Tea Sandwiches
Christmas Jewel Cookies
Turtle Dove Cheesecake Bars
Stuffed Apricots

INTRODUCTION
Welcome to Storyton Hall. I'm Jane Steward, Resort Manager, and I'd like to escort you to our Agatha Christie Tea Room. The rooms in our resort are all named after authors and, as you can see, each room is filled with books. Every day, we serve afternoon tea in the Agatha Christie Tea Room. Storyton Hall's cook, Mrs. Hubbard, lays a very fine table indeed. At Christmastime, she really outdoes herself. It might be cold outside, but it's warm and snug in our manor house. The tearoom smells of pine and cinnamon and hints of red, green, and white—the colors of Christmas—adorn the room. We've lined the fireplace mantel with gold pillar candles and dimmed the lights just a little to create an atmosphere of enchantment, because Christmas is a magical time a year. It can also be a very busy time for all of us. Believe me, I know. I'm a single mother with a very demanding job and I recognize the value and importance of taking the time to just sit—to gather around a table

with the people you love. So remember to invite a special friend or family member over for tea this holiday season. You'll be giving them a gift they'll never forget. The gift of a happy memory.

SETTING THE TABLE

At Storyton, we like to use crisp, white tablecloths as our tea table backdrop. For our Christmas tea, we strive to bring the natural environment inside, so the centerpiece of our tea tables begins with a pine wreath. This season, if you're planning to buy a wreath to hang on your front door, pick up a second wreath for your tea table. Set the wreath on the table and then place a white cake plate in its center. You'll put your tea service on the cake plate. The pine wreath will add a pleasant aroma to your room. You can leave it plain or add ribbons, ornaments, or other festive decorations to it. At Storyton, we tuck battery-operated tea lights between the needles. This creates a simple, but elegant effect. Next, we fold white cloth napkins lengthwise and tie them with red-and-white gingham ribbon. We slide a candy cane and a sprig of holly under the bow and place the napkins in the center of a white plate. If you'd like more color on your table, you could always add a red, green, or patterned runner, or placemats. You could also use Christmas-themed serving plates. No matter how you set your table, your guests are sure to be delighted by your tea party.

THE TEA

Black Tea with Orange Peel (served in a teapot).

To make dried orange peel, remove the peel from an orange. Next, scrape off as much as of the white, bitter pith as possible. Cut into thin pieces (about 1/8-inch thick) and spread on baking sheet lined with parchment paper. Toast in oven at 200°F (110°C, Gas Mark ¼) until completely dry; approximately 20 to 30 minutes. Dried orange peel can be refrigerated for up to 3 months. Use the peel from one orange to brew a pot of tea for your Christmas Tea. You might want more or less orange flavor in your tea, so making a test pot a week or two before your party is always a good idea.

DON'T FORGET THE FLOWERS

Abby Knight, from Kate Collins' Flower Shop Mysteries says....

Would Christmas be the same without mistletoe? White berried mistletoe is credited by ancient herbalists with curative powers, capable of alleviating everything from epilepsy to tumors. But beware of red mistletoe, which is poisonous. And of course Abby would have to include the holly and the ivy.

Flowers

Red roses

White spider mums

Celosia — magnificent plumes of bright red the celosia argentea, or Forest Fire

Mistletoe stems with white berries

Holly — white edged green leaves with red berries

Ivy (with black berries)

Container

A white toy sled with depth, a "gift box" covered with silver wrapping paper and tied with contrasting ribbon. Place shiny miniature glass ornaments in and around the centerpiece for accent.

RECIPES

Cranberry Chicken Salad Tea Sandwiches
Ingredients
¾ cup mayonnaise
2 tablespoons fresh lemon juice
1/3 cup fresh or frozen cranberries
½ small sweet onion, finely diced
2 tablespoons pecans, chopped
¼ teaspoon salt
¼ teaspoon pepper
3 cups cooked chicken, chopped fine
8 lettuce leaves
16 slices very thin bread, crusts removed (alternating dark and light bread makes for an attractive arrangement such as white and wheat or sourdough and pumpernickel)

Combine the first eight ingredients in a bowl. Layer half the slices of bread with lettuce. Spread the cranberry chicken salad over the lettuce and top with the remaining bread. Cut into triangles. Serve immediately.

Yield: 8 servings (32 triangle finger sandwiches)

Christmas Jewel Cookies
Ingredients
1 cup unsalted butter, softened
½ granulated sugar
1 large egg
1 teaspoon pure vanilla extract
½ teaspoon fresh lemon juice
2 ½ cups all-purpose flour, sifted
Several varieties of jam totaling about ½ cup. For Christmas colors, use apricot jam for gold, strawberry or seedless raspberry jam for red, and mint jelly for green.

Preheat the oven to 350°F (180°C, Gas Mark 4). Line 2 baking sheets with parchment paper. In a large bowl, cream the butter and sugar. Beat in the egg. Add in the vanilla extract and lemon juice. Gradually add the flour until completely blended. Roll the dough into 1-inch balls. Place 1 inch apart on the baking sheets. Press your finger into center of dough to form an indentation. Fill each depression with a little jam or jelly. Bake the cookies for 20 to 25 minutes, or until the edges are golden. Transfer to wire racks to cool. These cookies are so colorful that you can serve them on a plain white platter.

Yield: 3 to 4 dozen

Turtle Dove Cheesecake Squares
Crust
1/3 cup butter, softened
1/3 packed brown sugar
1 cup all-purpose flour, sifted

Filling
½ cup granulated sugar
2 8-ounce packages cream cheese, brought to room temperature
4 tablespoons whole milk
2 large eggs
1 teaspoon pure vanilla extract
1 cup semi-sweet chocolate chips

Topping
1 cup chopped pecans, toasted
caramel sauce
1 cup semi-sweet chocolate chips

Preheat the oven to 350°F. (180°C, Gas Mark 4). For pastry: Cream the butter and sugar. Gradually add the flour and stir until the mixture is crumbly. Press the mixture into an 8-inch square pan and bake for 12 to 15 minutes. While the crust is baking, prepare the filling.

For the filling: Beat sugar and cream cheese until smooth. Add the egg, milk, lemon juice, and vanilla and mix well. Remove the crust from the oven and sprinkle the chocolate chips over it. Spread the filling mixture over the layer of chocolate chips. Bake for 50 to 60 minutes or until the center rises and the pie filling doesn't jiggle. Cool on a wire rack and then refrigerate for at least one hour. (One day is preferable.) Cut into bars and drizzle each bar with caramel sauce. Garnish with pecans and chocolate chips.

Yield: 12 servings

Stuffed Apricots
Ingredients
1 cup mascarpone cheese
1¼ cups water
¾ cups superfine sugar
2 teaspoons fresh lemon juice
2 tablespoons honey
½ teaspoon cinnamon
1 pound dried whole apricots (the soft, ready-to-eat kind)
cinnamon to garnish

In a saucepan, over medium heat, bring water and sugar to a boil. Reduce heat, add lemon juice. Add the apricots to the water and let them simmer until they puff up (about 15 minutes). Using a slotted spoon, transfer the apricots to a baking sheet to cool. Mix the mascarpone, honey, and cinnamon in a bowl. Spoon the mixture into a piping bag. Locate hole in each apricot where stone was removed and, using a small knife, make the hole a little larger. Pipe the filling into each apricot. Arrange them on a platter. Serve at room temperature.

*If you're short on time, you can substitute canned halved apricots for dried apricots and spoon the filling directly on the fruit. Garnish with cinnamon.

Yield: 5 dozen

THE CHICK'S FOND MEMORIES OF TEA

"The famous 'art of tea' has been deeply impregnated with the spirit of Zen … as a 'way of spiritual experience.'"
—**Thomas Merton**, *American Catholic writer and mystic*

TEA MEMORIES

The Cozy Chicks have been sharing interesting tidbits and information about tea. And we've decided to include some of our most precious memories of tea, too. My contribution is an assortment of stray memories of "tea time" experiences in my life. I hope you enjoy them.
—*Maggie Sefton*

According to my father—who was born in Ireland and grew up in England—I first was introduced to black tea in my bottle. The story goes that at six months old I was crying with what was then referred to as "colic." After a couple of hours walking the floor, my father told my mother he was going to fix me a "good cuppa." My mother did not protest, probably due to exhaustion from walking the floor. I was still crying apparently. My father made some hot black tea (weaker than usual), then added some heaping spoonsful of sugar then poured in a generous portion of whole milk. Shaking it well and testing the temperature to make sure it was no longer hot, my father offered me the bottle. He said I took a taste, stopped crying, and drank the entire bottle. An early tea lover was born.

I've been drinking strong black tea ever since. Over my lifetime I've eliminated the sugar. Then several years later, I stopped adding milk. I discovered that I really, really enjoyed the flavor of strong black tea all by itself. Naked and unashamed. I start the day with hot black tea and still drink it into the evening. During the hotter weather I also drink iced tea. I've tried it with the fruit combinations, but still prefer the taste of tea alone. It's refreshing and cooling. Perfect for those hot and humid days I spend back east in Northern Virginia visiting family and friends.

To be fair to all tea drinkers, I also want to add a green tea memory. Back in January of 2003, I visited my daughter, Maria, who after college became a Lieutenant in the U.S. Navy on her first assignment and was aboard the USS KITTY HAWK, the oldest carrier in the Fleet. The "KITTY," as it was fondly called, was stationed at its home port in Yokasuka, Japan, in the Navy's Seventh Fleet. It was being repaired and readied for its next assignment.

Maria had a small apartment in Yokasuka (and in Japan, small means *small*), and I stayed with her for several days and explored Yokasuka before she and I took a vacation trip. We decided to take the train from Yokasuka all the way to the eastern part of the country to the historic city of Kyoto. We deliberately did not choose the Japanese "high speed" train and chose the local train which stopped at lots and lots of little towns as it took two days to reach Kyoto. We slept in our seats like everyone else and eagerly awaited the station stops where we raced off the train and into one of the little teeny "cafes."

In reality, they were tiny crowded rooms with counters and stools where customers perched and chose from the most gorgeous selection of sushi imaginable. We stuffed ourselves and drank from the constantly offered pot of hot green tea. To this day I have never tasted such delicious green tea. Perhaps it was the cold January weather, or the setting of the counters and stools and other hungry passengers, but Maria and I drank and ate more sushi, and drank some more and ate more sushi until we were stuffed. And at the next town, we would race into another cramped room filled with customers and eagerly hold our faces over a steaming bowl of fantastic noodles, again finished off with hot, delicious green tea. After reading Kate's piece on tea lore, I figure Maria and I must have been indulging in that wonderful Matcha green tea.

Oh, and Kyoto was as beautiful as everyone said it would be, even in January. We walked everywhere, and we even saw flowers blooming. In January.

"Afterwards, they always had tea in the kitchen, much the nicest room in the house."
—**Flora Thompson**, *English Novelist*

TEA WITH MY GRANDMOTHER
By Mary Jane Maffini

Allow me to tell you about my grandmother, Louise Ferguson Ryan. She was a tall, slim, elegant lady who was smart and funny and just a bit wicked. She's making an appearance here because she knew how to make a mean cup of tea.

One of the many benefits of this lovely tea book is that I've been thinking about her lately. In 1900 she was a teacher in a mountain village in rural Quebec, Canada. The story, as we kids were told, was that it was twenty-five miles up to the village and there were no cars, of course. She walked up on Sunday afternoon and back down again on Friday afternoon. In some versions, her brothers picked her up with the horses and wagon. I wonder if it was one of those roads, like the staircase in Fiddler on the Roof, with 'one long road going up and one even longer going down.' My grandmother was a gifted storyteller so all the versions sounded quite credible. After all, this was a woman who was left a widow with ten children, the youngest twins of a year, and the eleventh on the way. All eleven turned out to be handsome (or beautiful) funny, industrious, strong-minded and inclined to spin a tale or two.

The last summer we spent together, at the family cottage (somewhat grandly called The Lodge) on the gorgeous Restigouche River that runs between Quebec and the northern tip of New Brunswick, I was fourteen and she was eighty four. It worked for both of us. As a difficult teenager (short, round and freckled in a family of tall, elegant women with perfect skin), I was out of sorts a lot of the time. But on summer vacations, I could chat with my grandmother and avoid the critical aunties and most of the detested chores. She'd spin tales, share gossip, and spout poetry. Tennyson was a favorite and she knew many poems by heart. She loved Shakespeare, mystery, and intrigue. There were dozens of mysteries in bookcases at the cottage and we did talk about Agatha Christie, John Dixon Carr, and others of that ilk. No wonder I love writing the book collector mysteries (with my daughter under the name Victoria Abbott)! I go way back with that gang. The paperback mysteries are long gone, but I still have my grandmother's collection of "red" John Buchan hardbacks in my office.

Often we would just chill. She'd knit and I might chatter idly or try to learn 'fair isle' technique. As a leftie, I still haven't mastered it, but she never made me nervous about it. Whatever we did and whatever we talked and laughed about, we did it over hot tea.

I never spotted my grandmother in the kitchen except making tea. As the source of heat in the cottage was a large old wood stove, it was quite good news when some enterprising relative brought an electric kettle, as you really wanted to avoid that stove in the summer.

She taught me that first you 'hot the pot' with boiling water to make sure that teapot didn't lower the temperature of the finished cuppa. The water itself must be kept on what's affectionately known as 'the rolling boil.' We would transfer the water used to 'hot the pot' into a tin container so it could water tomato plants when it cooled. At our family lodge with water pumped from a spring, no one wasted a drop.

Two tea bags, Red Rose, of course, as this was Canada, were added to the pot and the boiling water added. We would wait exactly four minutes for it to steep and then remove the tea bags, pronto and with great drama! This produced a bracing brew that was perfect for sipping over book chat on the porch overlooking the sparkling river.

I often think of her when I'm having tea and feel grateful for the tea lessons and those early book chats. I have moved on to other teas, but the fun, closeness and book-talking companionship live on in happy memory. To this day, tea and talk with a friend is a happy and healing activity.

Thank you, Louise Ferguson Ryan, for all that and more.

"Tea is a blessing in disguise."
—**Alexandra Stoddard**, *American author*

AN AMERICAN IN YORKSHIRE
by Mary Kennedy

My first Yorkshire tea party was a memorable one. Picture this: a lovely red-brick Victorian house in a breathtaking setting in the north of England. The house was very close to the sea, and I caught a whiff of salt air, mixed with the delicious fragrance of honeysuckle and lavender. It was all wonderful and exciting to me because I was a visiting American, new to the country and new to the family.

I'd married a Brit and I found his family home to be formal, yet welcoming. As I made my way up the driveway, I noticed a greenhouse to the side of the house, some stables tucked away toward the back of the property and of course, a show-stopper English garden. What is it about English gardens that make them so spectacular? Is it all the rain? I wondered how to delicately ask that question without offending my hosts. On this afternoon, it was sunny in Yorkshire, with a gentle breeze rustling the leaves of the stately oaks that edged the path.

The setting was straight out of Masterpiece Theater, with women in summer dresses and straw hats, standing in small groups or seated at round tables that dotted the lawn. I learned later that most of the women were clustered outside, enjoying tea and pastries, while the men had retired to the house to imbibe something a bit stronger. Classical music was playing somewhere and the sound drifted over the expanse of the lush green lawn.

It was a peaceful scene; serene, perfect. There was only one jarring note. A large slab of concrete was placed smack dab at the far end of the garden, in front of some climbing roses and wisteria vines. How odd, I thought. I was determined to ask about it. But first I had to meet my new relatives! What would they think of this visiting American who had married into the family?

I needn't have fretted; I was welcomed with open arms and was quickly lost in a maze of introductions. Someone handed me a cup of tea and urged me to join them at a charming little table. (My husband had darted inside, presumably to drink some wonderful British ale or a mixed drink).

I knew that my mother-in-law was a great collector of vintage table linens, along with porcelain tea pots and I saw that each table had a unique setting. At my table, the covering was a creamy linen cloth, embroidered with miniature roses and green leaves along the border. I recognized the Royal Albert Old Country Roses tea set because another relative in Scarborough had exactly the same teapot.

As I settled in to enjoy the tea, a woman slipped into the seat next to me and handed me a plate filled with pastries. "I wasn't sure what you liked so I gave you a little bit of everything," she said with a shy smile. It turns out she was a family friend, invited to meet "Mary from America."

The talk turned to the delectable pastries and I quickly learned that my plate held rock buns, scones with clotted cream and strawberry jam, savory little cheese tarts, and tiny cucumber sandwiches. As if by magic, another plate appeared. It held a generous slice of sponge cake filled with raspberries and cream in the middle. "And you simply must try the Lemon Drizzle Cake," my new friend said. "It's a tradition. It's not a proper tea without Lemon Drizzle."

"I'll do my best," I promised.

More people came over to introduce themselves and

I learned about Yorkshire tea traditions. It seems English Trifle is served at tea, always in a glass bowl so you can see the different layers. The chunks of cake are soaked in sherry, the filling can be made with Bird's Custard (powder) if you're in a hurry (or home-made if you're not) and the fruit can be strawberries, blueberries or whatever you prefer. The cream is always "heavy cream" that's been whipped with a little sugar added.

The Trifle was kept in the kitchen, so it could be chilled. I didn't think it was possible to eat another bite, but I eventually made my way inside the house. I was warmly welcomed with white wine, sherry or a Shandy (beer mixed with carbonated lemonade.) I declined everything. I was eager to explore the stately old Victorian home and my mother-on-law had told me to "make myself at home."

As I checked out the sitting room with its beautiful moldings, gleaming wood floors and marble fireplace, I noticed there was a bell pull in the far corner. *Just like in Downton Abbey!* I couldn't resist giving it a tug. Naturally, no one appeared. I knew the house had a fourth floor designated for "servants' quarters," but the days of maids were long gone. I wandered into the book-lined study and came across another bell pull. I couldn't resist, I pulled that one, too! I took a peek at another sitting room and then made my way to the second floor where we would be staying. The dressing room had a bell pull and so did the guest bedroom. If only I'd lived a hundred years earlier, I'd never have to make my own tea again!

I was having fun with the bell pulls when my husband bounded up the stairs and said, "What in the world are you doing? Those bells are ringing off the hook in the kitchen, driving everyone crazy!"

Oh no! How embarrassing! I hadn't realized that every time I yanked on a bell pull, the bell went off in the kitchen where the men were gathered around an enormous refectory table. The kitchen, it seems, used to be the "servants' area," where the cook prepared meals and the staff gathered to eat their evening meals. The bell pulls were connected to flashing lights and ringers mounted on the wall above the sink. Apparently, the family members couldn't imagine what all the racket was until someone explained, "It's Alan's wife, Mary. She's wandering around the house, trying out the bells. She's an American."

Mortified, I quickly went downstairs and made my way out to the garden. I strolled down a sun-dappled path, admiring the Black-eyed Susans, moonflowers, delphinium, foxglove, and trumpet honeysuckle. There were bird baths and wrought iron benches, such an idyllic setting. And then I came across that strange concrete slab I'd noticed when I first arrived.

"You're probably wondering about that," a voice said. I turned to see one of my sisters-in-law who guided me to a nearby bench. "That's a bomb shelter," she said quietly. "We've never removed it. I know it seems like a bit of an eyesore, but somehow I like to see it and remember all the sacrifices that were made."

She went on to tell me about my husband's relatives who had fought in the war, about the children being evacuated from London and the terror of night bombings. She went on to talk about blackouts and rationing. Two uncles had fought in Germany; an aunt had been an ambulance driver for the troops.

A little chill went through me, and I suddenly appreciated this cold slab of concrete amidst the beauty of the flowers. It served as a stark reminder that England had been invaded, had suffered terrible losses, but had triumphed in the end.

"We have to stick together," she said, reaching out for my hand. "Brits and Americans. We're allies, you know."

"That we are," I said softly. "That we are."

Someone came over and asked us to play croquet just then and the somber mood was broken. Laughter and the tinkle of glasses drew me back to the bright sunny garden party. But I knew I would always remember my first Yorkshire tea and the mystery behind the concrete slab in the garden.

"When tea becomes ritual, it takes its place at the heart of our ability to see greatness in small things. Where is beauty to be found? In great things that, like everything else, are doomed to die, or in small things that aspire to nothing, yet know how to set a jewel of infinity in a single moment?"
—**Muriel Barbery,** *French novelist and professor of philosophy*

TEA WITH HIGH STYLE:
MEMORIES OF MUM
by Mary Jane Maffini

As a child, I loved my mother's tea parties. They were so dramatic. Better than television any old day and with much more suspense and glamor. She held them once a year in the fall, back to back, two days running, with about thirty-five women invited to each. The house would be in an uproar for days in preparation. Silver was polished until you could see your face in it. Tablecloths were starched and pressed so that not a line showed. China was taken from the cupboard and given another wash, just in case. You could smell the wax on the hardwood and a different wax for the furniture. Rugs were taken outside and beaten. If you were a strategic child, you would manage to stay out of the way to avoid tedious chores (polishing, washing dishes, and dusting) relating to the upcoming party, but contrived to reappear when there might be something fun to do. Or eat.

The kitchen was a hive of activity: baking, sandwich-making, pickle arranging, tea preparations and more. In the dining room, the Duncan Phyfe table would be open, both the leaves up, and covered with a white damask cloth. I used to think I could hear it groaning under the plates of party sandwiches (chicken, egg salad, salmon, and, yes, all crustless, so a big treat from my point of view) and plus the tiered dishes with shortbread, meringues, and cookies.

Back in the day, women received individual cups and saucers for wedding and shower gifts and my mother seemed to have more than her share. Today I still have many of them and others have gone to my daughters. We treasure them. Mum served her tea from her Spode Billingsley Rose teapots (there were two) and one special matching pot for hot water to top it up. Naturally, there was a matching sugar and cream set (although we would never serve cream with tea). I thought ladies were lucky if they got the perfect lacy Billingsley Rose cups.

My mother was always ready in plenty of time. I wish I had that gene. We'd be all dolled up and ready for the first peal of the doorbell. My mother would touch her hand to her impeccable chignon, touch her pearls, smooth her dress, and smile. We were 'away to the races.' The door would ring some thirty-five times. The ladies of course were part of the drama with their hats and gloves and best clothing and makeup. The dresses were fitted at the waist and had swirly skirts, courtesy of the crinolines popular at the time. I loved the swish of taffeta. It was the sound of a party to me. They smelled of eau de cologne, Chanel, or Emeraude, popular at the time. Their fur stoles were hung in the hall closet. There was chatter, laughter, and elegance. Of course, a bit of gossip always gave spice to the memories. Years later, I was to learn of some of the intrigue that went on, the feuds, the rumors, but those are tales for another time.

With luck, someone from the local paper would show up to take photos for the social pages. The photographer would always get the names right and include as many of the smiling ladies as possible. I remember them positioning themselves to the best advantage. Whoever poured the tea was acknowledged as this was quite an honor. At seven, I made the paper with the caption: "Miss Mary Jane Merchant poured." Given the child I was, I was lucky that a disaster didn't ensue.

I imagine that my mother felt some measure of triumph after the two 'teas' were over. She cared about her role in the community as she had married my father and come 'from away.' Thirty years later, she was still 'from away,' but her entertaining teas gave an idea of the style that could bring.

Good for you, Mum. You showed them how it was done.

Excerpts From Our Books

"Love and scandal are the best sweeteners of tea."
—**Henry Fielding**, *English novelist and dramatist*

SCENES FROM A HISTORICAL TEA
The Widow and the Rogue Mysteries
by Maggie Sefton

The following are two scenes from my Historical Mystery, SCANDALS, SECRETS AND MURDER: The Widow and the Rogue Mystery series. This mystery takes place in 1890 Washington, D.C. and has two sleuths working together—Amanda Duncan, an American widow who has psychic powers and Devlin Burke, a British investor and sometime-sleuth who is visiting his family in Washington and while there, helps his foolish nephew Freddie.

It seems Freddie has managed to become ensnared in a corrupt U.S. Senator's schemes and is now the chief suspect in the senator's brutal murder. Since Devlin is British and Amanda is from Washington Society, whenever a conversation is about to ensue, tea is always served. However, all of the conversations concern murder. Or, as the London Watch would call out: "Murder! Murder most foul!"

Scene #1

Devlin sat in the hansom cab and watched as Amanda Duncan stepped from her carriage and walked up the black wrought iron steps of her Washington, D.C. row house. He'd instructed the cabbie to park a little way down H Street so as not to be noticed. He observed the distinctive architectural details of Amanda Duncan's Federal style home, the decorative trim above the windows and door. Then the front door opened and Mrs. Duncan disappeared inside.

Deciding not to delay, lest he talk himself out of this even-more-improper act, Devlin withdrew a large bill from his wallet and exited the cab. The cabbie exclaimed his gratitude as Devlin headed toward the trim row house. Meanwhile, he rehearsed some rational explanation for following Amanda Duncan to her Jackson Square home. Discarding one reason after another, Devlin decided to rely on his instinct because it had never led him astray. He heaved the brass doorknocker twice.

After only a few seconds, the door opened to reveal a petite woman clad in a housemaid's long black dress and white frilled apron. A ruffled white lace cap held back her grey curls. Her bright, bird-like gaze swept over Devlin quickly.

"And who might you be, sir?" she asked in a heavy Irish brogue. Somehow, the elderly woman managed to look down her nose at Devlin even though she barely reached his chest.

Devlin smiled his most charming smile, hoping to thaw the diminutive servant's frosty attitude. "Good afternoon, madam. My name is Devlin Burke. Your mistress, Amanda Duncan, and I spoke earlier this morning regarding some business. Would you be so kind as to inquire if Mrs. Duncan has a moment to receive me? I have but one question to ask, and I promise I will be brief."

Devlin watched the frost turn to ice on the little maid's face. Her wrinkles froze in place. Once again, his British accent had sealed his fate. These American Irish seemed determined to dislike him.

"And what sort of business would you be discussing with my mistress, if you don't mind my askin'?" she inquired in a frigid tone.

Actually, Devlin did mind, but knew enough not to let on. He reached inside his vest pocked and, with flourish, handed her a calling card. "I am the financial advisor to my brother, the Earl of Devonshire and an here in Washington to oversee my family's investments. And to visit with my sister who is married to Jonathan Carrington, the junior senator from Maryland." Devlin hoped his favorable family connections would save him. Otherwise, the little maid might not allow him entry.

The maid frowned as she read the card. "Wait right here while I ask ..." Pausing, she turned her head as if listening. "Are you certain, madam?" she called behind her. Another pause. Then the maid turned to Devlin, and with an aggrieved sigh, opened the door to allow him entry. She held out her hand for his hat. "The parlor is down the hall and to your right, sir." Devlin couldn't miss the emphasis she placed on the word.

He gave her a gracious nod as well as his hat and strode down the hallway before the maid changed her mind. Devlin spied Amanda Duncan standing in the parlor, waiting for him. At least she wasn't scowling. He took that as a good sign and gave her his most gentlemanly bow.

"Mrs. Duncan, you are incredibly kind to receive me. Let me first apologize for my earlier breach of propriety. My concern for my nephew allowed me to temporarily forget my good manners, and for that, I am sincerely sorry."

"You are forgiven, Mr. Burke. We all go to great lengths to protect our families," Amanda said, gesturing to a midnight blue armchair. "Please have a seat."

Neither Devlin nor Amanda Duncan had the chance to sit, however, because the little Irish maid swept into the room. She fixed Devlin with a disapproving glare. "What's all this about breaching propriety and forgetting manners? Did this gentleman say something improper to you, madam?"

Devlin held his tongue and waited for Mrs. Duncan's answer. He wasn't about to open his mouth. He'd only put his foot in it.

"Not at all, Bridget," Amanda replied calmly. "He merely asked me a question as I was leaving the station house."

Instead of being appeased, Bridget stared at Devlin, clearly horrified. "Saints preserve us! You mean he approached you on the street without a proper introduction?"

Devlin did his best not to flinch under Bridget's withering glare. He could certainly feel its heat.

Amanda continued as calmly as before, as if she was used to her maid's emotional outbursts. "He did introduce himself, Bridget. And as you heard yourself, Mr. Burke is here in Washington to visit his family and conduct his business." Turning to Devlin, she gestured once more to the armchair. "Would you care for tea, Mr. Burke?"

Devlin gratefully sank into the inviting velvet. "Thank you, Mrs. Duncan. I would love some tea."

"Madam, I must protest," Bridget continued.

"There is no need, Bridget, I assure you. Now, go tell Matilda to prepare a tea tray for us, please," Amanda said, her tone calm, but firm.

Bridget glowered at Devlin once more, but did as she was bid, muttering none too softly, "Lord have mercy upon us all," as she left.

Amanda glanced at Devlin with a smile. "You must forgive my housekeeper. She's been with me since I was an infant. Consequently, she's fiercely protective. I fear I am too lax with her at times, but I simply cannot bring myself to scold her. I hope you weren't offended by her outburst."

"Not at all, Mrs. Duncan. Bridget was entirely in the right. My behavior was inexcusable outside the station house today. I deserved her tongue-lashing."

Amanda observed Devlin for a moment. "You said you had something to ask me, Mr. Burke. I'll be happy to answer if I can, but as I said earlier, I did not see the assailant's face in my vision. Just a shadowy dark figure."

This time Devlin chose his words carefully. "First, let me say that I completely understand your desire to protect the safety of the young girl who survived the attack. And I assure you, I have no intention of jeopardizing that safety. Not at all. I simply want to prove my nephew's innocence. And I thought the two of us could help each other with our mutual concerns."

Amanda looked at him with obvious interest. "How so?"

"You want to protect the girl from further harm, and I want to find the real killer of Senator Chester. If I succeed and the police arrest him, then the young girl will be safe forever."

Mrs. Duncan glanced toward the tall windows. Devlin followed her lead and glimpsed the President's House across the square and the avenue beyond. He also took the opportunity to glance around Amanda Duncan's elegantly appointed parlor. Moss green velvet draped the lace-curtained windows, a rich mahogany writing desk sat beside a corner window, and mahogany tables bordered a deep blue velvet settee. Walnut bookcases filled with volumes lined one wall, and gilt-edged oil paintings adorned the other walls.

"You make a good point, Mr. Burke," she said, returning her attention. "But I'm curious as to how I could help you in your search for Senator Chester's killer."

Devlin took a deep breath before answering. "I propose the two of us work together to search for clues as to this vicious killer's identity. I have a fair amount of detecting skills and have actually helped the constabulary in Devonshire ferret out wrongdoers. And I've interviewed several London investigators over the years. I believe that if we combine my analytical skills with your psychic abilities, we could uncover information that would lead us to the real perpetrator of this crime."

"I do not summon my clairvoyant visions, Mr. Burke.

They come unbidden whenever they choose. It is a gift that I receive, not a skill that I have mastered."

"I understand, Mrs. Duncan," Devlin continued, encouraged to see that he'd piqued Amanda Duncan's interest. He could tell from her expression. "But I have been present in London with other clairvoyants and psychics, and sometimes they receive additional visions when they are in the vicinity where a crime took place." He deliberately paused and watched her face. If shock replaced the curiosity, then Devlin knew he'd be ushered out before he even had a chance to drink his tea.

Amanda fixed her gaze on Devlin. "What are you suggesting, Mr. Burke?" she asked in a quiet voice.

Devlin paused before answering, making sure his voice was as calm as hers. "Would you be willing to accompany me to the scene of Senator Chester's murder? Perhaps you could sense something more of the killer's identity."

Amanda stared at Devlin, her eyes wide, not saying a word. Devlin held his breath, praying that she would agree. Her face didn't reveal a trace of emotion, save surprise.

"Are you familiar with the area of Washington where the crime occurred, Mr. Burke?"

"Yes, Mrs. Duncan, I believe it happened in a rather unsavory neighborhood called Murder Bay. Trust me, I shall ensure that you will not be exposed to any disreputable characters. I propose we visit the, uh . . . establishment during the morning hours when the likelihood of the most objectionable persons being present would be considerably—"

"Holy Mother and all the Saints! I cannot believe my ears!" Bridget's sharp voice sliced through the room. The little housekeeper stood in the archway where she'd obviously been listening. "Madam, I knew he was no gentleman! Not at all—at all. To make such a wicked suggestion! He is a knave, to be sure. I recognize a rogue when I see one. Even one disguised in expensive Savile Row tailoring."

"Now, Bridget," Amanda soothed.

Devlin had to give Bridget credit. Her eye was as sharp as her tongue. But this time he decided he simply must defend his honor as a gentleman. He leaned forward in the chair, his hand on his breast.

"Mrs. Duncan, I swear to you, my suggestion was entirely innocent of any base motives. I seek only the truth in this tragic event. And I would never expose you to any situations which would cause you distress—"

"HA!" Bridget scoffed, fists on her hips.

"Bridget, that is enough," Amanda said in a firm tone. "I believe Mr. Burke's intentions are entirely honorable. His motive is solely to prove his nephew's innocence. He's simply trying to search out the identity of Senator Chester's murderer. And for that, he needs my help."

Bridget turned to her mistress, clearly appalled. "Madam! You cannot be serious. You simply cannot set foot in that wretched area of the city."

"It seems Mr. Burke and I have mutual goals, Bridget. I want to ensure that young girl's future safety. Mr. Burke wants to clear his nephew of police suspicion by finding the real culprit." She glanced to Devlin. "If I help him in that endeavor, then both goals will be assured."

Devlin couldn't believe what he was hearing. Amanda Duncan was obviously considering his suggestion. "Absolutely, Mrs. Duncan—"

Bridget cut him off again. "Madam! Might I remind you that your reputation has already been tarnished by your work with the good Sisters of Saint Anne's. Going with them into those filthy tenements is horrible enough, but this—" She gestured wordlessly for a change.

Devlin saw his chance and took it. "Bridget, I assure you that I am sensitive to your mistress's situation. That's why I am proposing that we make this foray as brief as possible and in the early morning hours, when the reprobates are off the streets. Secondly, I suggest that Mrs. Duncan disguise herself by wearing a hooded cloak, which would conceal her identity from all curious eyes."

Bridget was apparently taken by surprise at Devlin's suggestion. However, he glimpsed a hint of a smile from Amanda Duncan.

"You see, Bridget. Mr. Burke's intentions are completely above board. Plus, he has made an eminently practical suggestion. I have decided to help him with his investigation." She glanced to Devlin. "When do you suggest we make this trek into the nether regions, Mr. Burke? I have tomorrow morning free."

"Tomorrow would be perfect, Mrs. Duncan," Devlin replied, elated at her cooperation. Glancing to a clearly fuming Bridget, he decided it would be wise to provide insurance. So he addressed the outraged housekeeper. "Why don't you accompany us, Bridget? That way you will be able to assist me in my efforts to protect your mistress. The two of us will provide a formidable defense against any and all reprobates."

Clearly taken aback, Bridget stared at him, then her mistress.

"That's an excellent idea," Amanda chimed in. "You'll come with us, won't you, Bridget?"

Straightening herself taller, Bridget regained some of her bluster. "Of course, I will, madam."

"Excellent. It is settled, then." Devlin spied another servant approach bearing a silver tray. Afternoon tea.

"Thank you, Matilda," Amanda said to the woman with skin the color of honey. "Your timing is perfect. Mr. Burke and I have just negotiated a challenging business venture."

"Hmmmmh!" Bridget gave a derisive shrug, then went to clear a place for the tray. There, she busied her self with the tea service.

Once Amanda and Devlin had both been served, Amanda held up her cup to Devlin and smiled. "Congratulations on a successful negotiation, Mr. Burke."

Devlin responded in kind. "To diplomacy, Mrs. Duncan."

Scene #2

"Good afternoon, Mr. Burke," Amanda greeted Devlin as he entered her parlor. "Please have a seat. Bridget, please tell Matilda we'll have tea."

"I'm glad I found you at home, Mrs. Duncan, I have much to share with you." Devlin walked to his favorite velvet armchair, directly across from Amanda's. "Much has happened since we were last together."

"Yes, I sensed you had something to tell me, but Sister Beatrice's appearance prevented it."

Devlin let out a sigh. "Chief Inspector Donnolly arrived to question our nephew, Freddie. And today, Jonathan has conferred with his attorney to represent Freddie. We expect Inspector Callahan will file charges in a few days for Senator Chester's murder. And young Francie's." Noticing Amanda's shocked expression, Devlin leaned forward in his chair and implored, hand over his heart. "Mrs. Duncan, I cannot believe Freddie killed Senator Chester. And I would swear on my sister's life that Freddie could never kill that innocent girl." He implored Amanda, who still had a wary look in her eyes.

"Why, then, is Inspector Callahan filing charges?" Amanda asked her expression skeptical. "He may be boorish, but Callahan is not a careless man. He must believe there's enough evidence to convict your nephew."

Devlin sank back in his chair. "Alas, all the evidence is circumstantial. But because of Freddie's intemperate behavior with Chester, attacking him in the Senate hallway in front of witnesses, Freddie seems the likeliest suspect. Freddie is the only one who has no explanation for his whereabouts at the time of both murders. He was asleep at the Willard while Chester was killed."

"And where was he the night of Francie's murder?"

Devlin looked into her wary gaze and let her see his anxiety. "I left the convent that night and went straight to the Willard to check on Freddie and found that he had taken a walk. about the city—alone."

"I see," Amanda said, her eyes revealing a concern that Devlin had not seen since he first spoke with Amanda Duncan in her carriage outside the precinct station house.

"I understand your suspicion, Mrs. Duncan. And if I didn't know Freddie so well, I would believe him guilty, too. But, he is simply not that calculating."

Devlin stopped as Matilda brought the tea tray. He spied two slices of cake beside the teacups, and his stomach growled. Devlin had completely forgotten about the time, now his hunger demanded attention. He watched Amanda pour a double serving of cream into his tea. He accepted the cup eagerly and tried not to down it in one gulp.

"I see your point about Chester's murder, Mr. Burke. But what of Francie's?" Amanda questioned. "You must admit your nephew's long walk alone that night leads one to make the assumption that he did indeed kill her."

Devlin drained his cup. "I agree it looks very bad, but Freddie simply could not have killed Francie. Whoever did kill that poor girl thought through the crime carefully and deliberately planned how to lure the priest and sisters away from the convent so that he could do his dark deed. But the truth is, Mrs. Duncan, Freddie is simply not that smart," Devlin declared. "I swear he is not. To be perfectly blunt, Freddie is just shy of being stupid." Devlin sank back in the chair, dejected. Listening to himself try to convince Amanda of Freddie's innocence made Devlin realize how unbelievable it sounded.

Amanda handed him a dessert plate. "You have that

lean and hungry look, Mr. Burke. Here, have some of Matilda's Louisiana rum cake. It's quite good. I'll pour you another cup of tea."

Devlin accepted the plate and scented the enticing aromas of rum and sugar wafting to his nostrils. His stomach growled so loudly, he was afraid Mrs. Duncan might hear it. "Thank you," was all he managed before he took a bite. *Heavenly.* Devlin closed his eyes and savored. "Delicious does not do this justice," he said after taking another large bite.

"Yes, it is delicious," Amanda said, placing another cup of tea at his elbow. "Now, let us assume for the moment that your belief about your nephew is true, and Freddie did not commit the murder. How can you convince Inspector Callahan of his innocence? Have you learned anything new from your meetings? I believe you were going to meet with another Senator, correct? Someone Jonathan suggested, I believe."

Devlin polished off the last bite of cake and licked his lips. "Yes, I met with Senator George Smythe this morning, and I learned something which has aroused my interest considerably."

Amanda sipped her tea. "Senator Smythe is an honorable man. I've met him and his family. What did he say that caught your interest?"

"He told me that Senator Chester and Senator Remington, had a heated argument only a month ago. Smythe accidentally overheard the entire exchange. Chester wanted Remington to step aside so the Governor could appoint someone else to the Senate. Someone Chester favored more. Remington refused and became quite emotional, pleading with Chester not to push him aside. But Chester told him to retire and be wealthy, or refuse and be ruined." Devlin took a deep drink of tea, and glanced toward the second slice of cake. "Smythe added that Remington was in a foul mood for days afterwards."

Amanda eyed him. "Are you suggesting that Edmund Remington killed Chester?"

Devlin released a long breath. "I believe it is a strong possibility. And, there's more that leads me to that conclusion." He glanced toward the cake again.

"Please have another piece, Mr. Burke," Amanda said, smiling as she gestured to the tray. "I'll have Matilda bring more."

Devlin hesitated. "Wouldn't you like it?"

"I've had Matilda's cake for a lifetime," she said with a wry smile. "Go ahead. Enjoy yourself. Matilda's a fine cook."

Devlin accepted her offer and tried not to gobble down another delectable bite, but the brown sugar and buttery taste tempted him to forget his manners. "This is delectable," he said after swallowing.

"Yes, isn't it?" Amanda said from behind her teacup. "Bridget, would you ask Matilda to bring the rest of the cake, please?"

"The entire cake?" Bridget asked, in surprise. Glancing to Devlin, she wagged her head before leaving.

Chagrined, Devlin had to smile. "Leave it to Bridget to make me remember my good manners. Forgive me for acting like a ravenous beast."

"You were clearly hungry, Mr. Burke. I rather enjoy watching someone else savor Matilda's fine cooking. Now, you were about to tell me something else that roused your suspicions about Edmund Remington."

Devlin licked brown sugar from his upper lip and proceeded to explain his theories why he believed Senator Remington killed Horace Chester. Amanda Duncan listened attentively through Devlin's entire recitation. Then she glanced out the window looking out onto Jackson Square. After a moment she turned back to Devlin and said in a sympathetic tone.

"I understand that all the evidence against your

nephew Freddie is circumstantial, but that is also true of Edmund Remington. And, I hate to say it, Mr. Burke, but Senator Remington would never arouse Inspector Callahan's suspicions, even if Callahan learned of Senator Smythe's overheard conversation, whereas, Freddie's own actions have caused him to look guilty."

What slight elation Devlin might have felt at Mrs. Duncan's initial praise, disappeared as quickly as air from a child's broken rubber balloon. Deflated, he distracted himself with Matilda's entrance carrying another full tea tray. Half a Louisiana Rum cake sat temptingly with two slices already on the plates.

"Alas, I'm forced to admit you are right, Mrs. Duncan," Devlin said, dejectedly. "Smythe's overheard conversation between Remington and Chester had bolstered my belief that Remington is the killer. But, alas, we have no way to prove it. And I agree, Remington would never be suspected as long as Freddie is such an attractive target." He glanced toward the tea tray again.

"Matilda's cake is a wonderful balm for many sorrows, Mr. Burke," Amanda suggested with a warm smile. "I'm sorry if I was blunt. May I suggest another piece?"

Devlin glanced toward the tempting cake again. He could swear he smelled the brown sugar and butter. "I really shouldn't. Three pieces would be entirely too much."

"It doesn't sound as if you had time for lunch, Mr. Burke. Why don't you make Matilda's cake your midday meal?"

Devlin chuckled as he retrieved another luscious slice of cake. "You would have made an excellent barrister, Mrs. Duncan. You're quite persuasive."

"Why, thank you, Mr. Burke. I find that talent is rather useful." She smiled as she poured another cup of tea.

Devlin let the luscious flavors of brown sugar, butter, and rum dissolve on his tongue. Divine.

"I had the strangest dream last night, Mr. Burke," Amanda said, staring out into the parlor. "I was in an unfamiliar house, and there was a large grandfather clock standing against the wall. The glass case was open, and the hands of the clock were moving backward. I do not know what to make of it."

Devlin set his fork on the plate and took a sip of tea, picturing the image Amanda had described. "Perhaps it means that time is running out for Freddie," he said grimly.

Scandals, Secrets And Murder is available in all e-book formats: Kindle, Kindle Worldwide, Nook, Kobo, iBooks, Smashwords

"Tea's proper use is to amuse the idle, and relax the studious, and dilute the full meals of those who cannot use exercise, and will not use abstinence."
—**Samuel Johnson**, *Essay on Tea, 1757*

Excerpt from
THE ICING ON THE CORPSE
A Camilla MacPhee Mystery
by Mary Jane Maffini

In this scene from The Icing on the Corpse, the second book featuring lawyer and victims' rights activist, Camilla MacPhee mystery, Camilla has no choice but to visit Alvin Ferguson— the world's worst office assistant, free spirit, and general pain in the backside—to get help with her case. Her client has been accused of murdering an abusive ex- and all the wrong people seem to be in trouble with the police, including Camilla. Still, all the drama distracts Camilla from the horrible fact that she's supposed to be a bridesmaid at her sister's wedding and it's time to—gulp—pick out a dress.

Half an hour later, I pulled my rental car in front of the scruffy building in the heart of old Hull. The Chateau Alvin, as I thought of it. He didn't answer his phone. For once, he was doing what I told him. I didn't feel like waiting until he picked up my latest voice mail message.

I followed a child in a bulky snowsuit and a tuque in through the supposedly locked front door and sniffed the illicit substances in the air. Alvin was home and probably still sulking. After two minutes of steady knocking, the door opened a finger's width.

Alvin said, "What, out of the slammer already?"

"I want to come in. I'll explain what's happening and you can decide whether or not you want to help me or whether you want to continue to bitch about perceived slights."

The child who had been watching our exchange like it was a game lost interest when I took a step through the door. Just in time, I remembered my last visit, and I gripped the door frame to keep from falling into darkness.

"You don't have to do that anymore," Alvin said, "I've redecorated."

Jimmy Buffett music should have been my first clue. Alvin's bathing suit with the watermelon motif should have been the second. The floors of the apartment had disappeared under a warm carpet of sand. Where there had been walls, an endless aqua ocean flowed, converging with clear blue sky up toward the ceiling.

"Where did you get the sand?"

"Here and there," Alvin said obliquely. "Artists have to be resourceful."

If I had to count my blessings, I'd put not being Alvin's landlord close to the top of the list.

Within a minute, beads of sweat had formed on my forehead. I slipped out of my parka and boots. I draped the parka over the nearest palm tree and propped the boots in front of the beer cooler. I slumped into a striped beach chair.

The only familiar landmarks were Alvin's big old fridge in the middle of the living room and the toilet with the plant growing out of it. The last time I'd been here it had been an ivy plant. This was bougainvillea.

It might kill me being nice to Alvin, but I knew there was no other way. I needed a bigtime payoff, so I made the first investment.

"I'm sorry, Alvin, for the bad things that have happened to you. I realize I'm not always the easiest person to deal with."

His bony shoulders relaxed. "I guess you had a bad day, getting charged. Hey! How about a margarita?"

I shook my head. All I needed was a snootful of

tequila to scramble my brain. "I need a cup of tea."

"Hibiscus tea?"

"No, thanks."

"Papaya-Mango tea?"

I didn't believe there was any such thing, but I wanted to be on the safe side. "Regular please. Like your mother would make."

Alvin loped across the sand dune and into the clear blue sea to the kitchen. He is one of those people who can talk and lope at the same time.

I made myself comfortable, peeled off my red socks and wiggled my toes in the sand while Alvin made the tea. I spent the next few minutes speculating about how he managed to warm the sand.

Alvin finally showed up bearing a silver tray and the pink flowered tea pot and matching cups and saucers I knew had belonged to his grandmother. This time I was impressed to note he had sugar cubes with a small silver set of tongs to serve them. It might have been a bit formal for the beach if it hadn't been for the little umbrellas in each cup.

I put four sugar cubes in my tea, which was hot, strong and black in the best Cape Breton tradition.

Then I filled him in on the scene at the police station.

"Wow. Elaine contacted the police to have a harassment charge laid against you?"

"Yep. And they took her seriously."

"Is it serious?"

"You bet. If it gets past the preliminary hearing and goes to trial, it will be."

"They couldn't convict you."

"Life has been full of surprises these past few days, Alvin. The usual 'couldn'ts' don't apply."

Alvin scratched his head. "Why wouldn't the other people at WAVE try to talk sense to her?"

"You tell me, Alvin. None of it makes any sense. It's a

high price to pay for some media profile. Most people draw the line at murder as a tactic."

"For once, you might be right."

"Even more troubling is the issue of the police and what they have to hide. And who they want to protect. They're willing to let an innocent person get sent jail to protect someone. Listen to this: I haven't had a chance to tell you yet, but Lindsay says Benning's police contact was a woman."

Most gratifying. Alvin came close to dropping his heirloom cup.

I continued. "I wonder if it might not be the same female cop who followed me to the door of the cop shop less than an hour before I was attacked. Maybe she has some connection to this Randy Cousins. Maybe they work together or they're partners."

"Uh-oh. I can see where you're headed."

"Yep. If I do what I have to and help Elaine help herself, I'm headed for jail, same as her."

"What do you need me to do? Go out to the Regional Detention Center and talk to her?"

I didn't give this a thought. "Too dangerous, Alvin. As my employee, you are bound by the *no contact* conditions. I'd get clapped in the slammer and you'd be right behind me."

Alvin kicked at the sand. "I don't want to get arrested again."

"Can't say I blame you. But what I have in mind won't lead to any problems for you."

He lifted his sunglasses and stared at me, unblinking. "Are you sure this time?"

"Trust me."

He rolled his eyes. "Fine, Camilla. Tell me what you want me to do."

"Find me Randy Cousins and get a name for our female officer. Priority One. I'm beginning to ask myself if they're in it together."

Alvin said. "I'll call in the reserves."

This excerpt from The Icing on the Corpse: a Camilla MacPhee mystery is posted by arrangement with Dundurn Press. Copyright © 2001 by Mary Jane Maffini

The Icing on the Corpse *is available in paperback and all e-book formats.*

"The proper, wise balancing of one's whole life may depend upon the feasibility of a cup of tea at an unusual hour."
—**Arnold Bennett**, *author of* How to Live on 24 Hours a Day

Excerpt from
A CRAFTY KILLING
A Victoria Square Mystery
by Lorraine Bartlett

The last thing Katie Bonner wanted was to become the manager of Artisans Alley. But when her business partner, Ezra Hilton, is found lying at the bottom of a staircase, bludgeoned to death, she has no other choice. A collection of booths for artisans and craft sellers in a renovated applesauce factory building, Artisans Alley is the main attraction in the quaint Victoria Square shopping area. But business under Ezra had been faltering. While the cops are proceeding by the book, Katie is investigating by the booths—for the answer to the killer's identity lies in the hidden secrets of Artisans Alley itself.

Katie snuck out of Artisans Alley's back entrance and threaded her way through the cars in Victoria Square's parking lot, heading for Tea and Tasties. When the heavenly scent of baking met her halfway, she breathed deeply and quickened her pace.

The brunch crowd was long gone and the shop's front door was locked. The darkened storefront looked anything but welcoming, but a car parked at the side of the building told her that someone was still inside. Katie went around to the back of the store and knocked on the door marked DELIVERIES.

Wiping her damp palms on the back of her jeans, Katie rocked on her heels, waiting for someone to answer.

Over the years she'd lost contact with old friends. Thanks to their full-time jobs, Katie's schoolwork, and Chad's booth at Artisans Alley, the couple had scant time to build or maintain outside friendships. Since Chad's death, Katie had occupied herself working long hours at Kimper Insurance with little time for anything else—with the exception of her baking hobby, that is. Now, when she really needed it, her support system was definitely lacking. Had Tracy's invitation the evening before only been polite conversation? The thought depressed her.

Finally the door rattled open. Mary Elliott greeted her, wiping her hands on her apron. "Hello, Katie. Tracy said you might stop by, but we were expecting you much sooner."

"I was detained," Katie said simply, grateful for the cheerful welcome.

Mary frowned. "Yes, we saw the police cars. Please, come in."

Katie stepped into the cocoon of warm air, her eyes wide with envy as she took in the banks of ovens on the far wall. The kitchen's center island work station contained sacks of opened flour and sugar, bowls of separated eggs, and tubs of spices. Despite the chaos of the work area, the rest of the room was spotless. A rack of trays stood nearby, filled with fresh-baked cookies. Envy burned within her. Oh, if she could only have such a wonderful kitchen to bake in.

"I think I've died and gone to heaven," Katie said, and took in yet another deep lungful of the heavenly aromas.

Mary pursed her lips, swallowing. Katie had forgotten the poor woman had found Ezra's body just two days before. Swallowing down guilt, and not wanting to bring more attention to her stupid remark, she asked for Tracy.

Mary stepped over to the wall and pressed a button. A harsh bell sounded in some other part of the converted house. Moments later Tracy appeared, dressed in tight jeans, a bulky blue sweater, and black suede high-heeled boots, looking comfortable, yet smart. "Glad you could make it, Katie. Have you had lunch?" she asked.

"As a matter of fact, no. And after everything that happened this morning, I could sure use a pick-me-up." Did that sound like too blatant a plea for a freebie? And truthfully, Katie felt that a shot of whiskey was more likely to hit the spot, but she didn't voice the idea.

"You're in the right place for tea and sympathy," Tracy said, her voice welcoming. "Come on into the shop."

"Put the kettle on, Tracy. The walnut scones will be out of the oven in a few minutes," Mary said, and went back to her work.

Mary had been occupied with customers the day before, so Katie had only told her about the vendors' meeting before hurrying on to Nona Fiske's quilt shop. Now she had a real opportunity to study the shop, and was absolutely delighted. Several small tables, with seating for two or four, lined the west wall. Linen covered, each table held a bud vase with a pink or red carnation and a spray of baby's breath. The opposite wall housed a large refrigerated case, filled with all sorts of tempting sweets, a counter, and a lovely antique cash register. Dainty rose-patterned wallpaper decorated the walls, with a teacup border edging the ceiling. An old oak schoolhouse clock told Katie it was already after three. Shelf upon shelf of floral teapots and matching cups or mugs, tea cozies, and toast racks were available for sale, as were the packages of imported blended teas Tracy had mentioned the day before.

"The scuttlebutt is Artisans Alley had a break-in overnight," Tracy said, and moved behind the counter.

"That's true. My office was ransacked. There's no telling if the burglar found what he was looking for."

"This is getting downright scary. That's why I insisted

on being here this afternoon. I don't want Mom working here alone anymore." Tracy sighed. "Do you have a tea preference?"

Katie shook her head. "Anything's fine."

Tracy grabbed a teapot from one of the shelves. "How about Earl Grey? It's my favorite."

Katie nodded, taking in the soothing atmosphere, something she'd hoped to convey if or when she opened the English Ivy Inn. "Your shop is lovely. It makes me want to pull out my checkbook and buy everything in sight."

Tracy smiled. "That's just the ambiance we'd hoped for."

"Of course, the reality is—" Katie started.

"You don't have to tell me," Tracy said. "Discretionary spending has been on the wane for a long while now. That's why Mom still takes on the occasional catering order. She's working on one now. We had a rough first year, but we're already pulling in a modest profit. I'm praying that continues."

Was that yet another veiled reminder that Victoria Square's merchants were dependent on Artisans Alley for their survival?

Katie took a seat and stared at the wooden tabletop. "By any chance do you have time to listen to a sob story?"

Tracy's smile was warm. "All the time you need."

While Tracy made the tea, Katie poured out her troubles, starting with the break-in, and backtracking to her heated discussion with Gerald Hilton the evening before. She even told Tracy about her job at Kimper Insurance, and how unhappy she was with the way Josh treated her.

Tracy served the steaming brew in delicate, primrose-patterned bone china cups. "Sorry about your day job, and it sounds like Gerald hasn't got a leg to stand on. Serves him right for being so mean to the artists."

Mary joined them, bringing in a tray laden with still-warm scones piled on a three-tiered plate, sweet butter, raspberry jam, and clotted cream to the table. She served, placing a paper-doily-covered plate before each of them.

"I don't know what I'm going to do about a manager for Artisans Alley," Katie said. "I don't know anyone else who's qualified to take over, or even who I can trust. I guess I'll have to call an employment agency." She took a bite of the warm, crumbly confection, savored it, and swallowed. Good as it was, it couldn't hold a candle to the scones her beloved Aunt Lizzie had made.

"Why don't you take charge yourself?" Mary asked, adding a dollop of clotted cream to her scone.

"Me? There's no way. I have a real job."

"A job you don't really like," Tracy added. "And it sounds like you're vastly overqualified for it, as well. You ought to make use of that marketing degree of yours."

"I tried getting jobs in the field, but all the big Rochester firms keep downsizing and firing—not hiring—workers. Besides, I have no practical experience in marketing. At least at Kimper Insurance I have health care and other benefits."

"Like what?" Mary asked.

"Vacation, for one."

"Which your boss gives you a hard time about using," Tracy reminded her.

"Working for Josh Kimper isn't the best job in the world," Katie admitted, "but it's stability. I can't possibly give it up for Artisans Alley. Especially when I don't even know if I can keep the place afloat until Christmas—let alone beyond."

Mary put a hand on Katie's shoulder. "You don't have to make up your mind today, dear. Think about it tomorrow when Artisans Alley is closed." She glanced at the clock. "Oops. I've got some mocha-chocolate chip cookies in the oven. They're due to come out right about now." As if on cue, a bell rang in the kitchen. Mary rose from her seat and hurried off.

"Did you see Ezra's death notice in the paper this morning?" Katie asked, referring to the announcement notice Seth had placed in the Democrat and Chronicle.

Tracy nodded. "In case you didn't know, Mother and Ezra were . . . friends."

"Good friends?" Katie asked.

"Close friends," Tracy clarified, and Katie remembered Mary's sobs upon finding Ezra—her lover?—dead.

"If she'd like some private time with Ezra before the burial, I'd be happy to arrange it."

Tracy's gaze darted to the kitchen then back to Katie. "I'll let you know. Thank you."

"Artisans Alley closes in about an hour. I'd better get back." Katie stood and started for the door, but then she turned. "Thanks for the tea—and the sympathy."

"I'll see you at the funeral home tomorrow night," Tracy said.

Katie headed for the door, and then stopped abruptly, her throat suddenly dry. The memory of Ezra's still body stretched out on Artisans Alley's floor filled her mind. "Oh my God," she breathed. "Ezra's really dead." She turned her tear-filled eyes toward Tracy.

Without hesitation, Tracy stepped forward and embraced her, patting her back sympathetically.

"I don't know why it hit me like this," Katie said, wiping at her eyes. "But suddenly I just feel so alone."

"You can handle this. It's not the end of your world. It's a new beginning," Tracy suggested.

"It's a beginning all right, but of what?"

Tracy didn't answer, just patted Katie's back some more.

"I'm sorry," Katie apologized and pulled away. "I didn't mean to dump on you like this."

Tracy smiled with a look of distant pain in her own

eyes. "It's okay. What're friends for?"

*A **Crafty Killing** is available in paperback and all e-book formats.*

"Tea is the magic key to the vault where my brain is kept."
—**Frances Hardinge**, *author*

Excerpt from
MURDER IN THE MYSTERY SUITE
A Book Resort Mystery
by Ellery Adams

Storyton Hall caters to book lovers who want to get away from it all. To increase her bookings, manager Jane Steward has decided to host a Murder and Mayhem week for some role-playing and fantasy crime solving. But when the winner is found dead in the Mystery Suite, and the valuable book that he won is missing, Jane realizes that one of her guests is an actual murderer. Amid a resort full of fake detectives, Jane is bound and determined to find a real-life killer.

Chapter 1

There were books everywhere. Hundreds of books. Thousands of books. There were books of every size, shape, and color. They lined the walls from floor to ceiling, standing straight and rigid as soldiers on the polished mahogany shelves, the gilt lettering on their worn spines glinting in the soft light, the scent of supple leather and aging paper filling the air.

To Jane Steward, there was no sweeter perfume on earth. Of all the libraries in Storyton Hall, this was her favorite. Unlike the other libraries, which were open to the hotel's paying guests, this was the personal reading room of her great-uncle Aloysius and great-aunt Octavia.

"Are you ready, Sinclair?" Jane mounted the rolling book ladder and looked back over her shoulder.

A small, portly man with a cloud of white hair and ruddy cheeks wrung his hands in agitation. "Oh, Miss Jane. I wish you wouldn't ask me to do this. It doesn't seem prudent."

Jane shrugged. "You heard what Gavin said at our last staff meeting. The greenhouse is in disrepair, the orchard needs pruning, the hedge maze is overgrown, the folly is hidden in brambles, and the roof above the staff quarters is rotting away. I have to come up with funds somehow. Lots of funds. What I need, Sinclair, is inspiration." She held out her arms as if she could embrace every book in the room. "What better place to find it than here?"

"Can't you just shut your eyes, reach out your hand, and choose a volume from the closest shelf?" Sinclair stuck a finger under his collar, loosening his bow tie. Unlike Storyton's other staff members, he didn't wear the hotel's royal blue and gold livery. As the resort's head librarian, he distinguished himself by dressing in tweed suits every day of the year. The only spot of color that appeared on his person came in the form of a striped, spotted, floral, or checkered bow tie. Today's was canary yellow with prim little brown dots.

Jane shook her head at the older gentleman she'd known since childhood. "You know that doesn't work, Sinclair. I have to lose all sense of where I am in the room. The book must choose me, not me, it." She smiled down at him. "Ms. Pimpernel tells me that the rails have recently been oiled, so you should be able to push me around in circles with ease."

"In squares, you mean." Sinclair sighed in defeat. "Very well, Miss Jane. Kindly hold on."

Grinning like a little girl, Jane gripped the sides of the ladder and closed her eyes. Sinclair pushed on the ladder, hesitantly at first, until Jane encouraged him to go faster, faster.

"Are you quite muddled yet?" he asked after a minute or so.

Jane descended by two rungs but didn't open her eyes. "I think I'm still in the Twentieth-Century American Authors section. If I'm right, we need to keep going."

Sinclair grunted. "It's getting harder and harder to confuse you, Miss Jane. You know where every book in this library is shelved."

"Just a few more spins around the room. Please?"

The ladder began to move again. This time, however, Sinclair stopped and started without warning and changed direction more than once. Eventually, he succeeded in disorientating her.

"Excellent!" Jane exclaimed and reached out her right hand. Her fingertips touched cloth and leather. They traced the embossed letters marching up and down the spines for a few brief seconds, before traveling to the next book. "Inspire me," she whispered.

But nothing spoke to her, so she shifted to the left side of the ladder, stretching her arm overhead until her hand brushed against a book that was smaller and shorter than its neighbors. "I believe you have something to tell me," she said and pulled it from the shelf.

Sinclair craned his neck as if he might be able to read the title from his vantage point on the ground. "Which one chose you, Miss Jane?"

"A British mystery," she said, frowning. "But I don't see how—"

At that moment, two boys burst into the room, infusing the air with screams, scuffles, and shouts. The first, who had transformed himself into a knight using a stainless steel salad bowl as a helmet and a gray T-shirt covered with silver duct tape as armor, brandished a wooden yardstick. The second boy, who was identical to the first in every way except for his costume, wore a green raincoat. He had the hood pulled up and tied under his chin and he carried two hand rakes. His lips were closed around a New Year's Eve party favor, and every time he exhaled, its multicolored paper tongue would uncurl with a shrill squeak.

"Boys!" Jane called out to no effect. Her sons dashed around chairs and side tables, nearly overturning the coffee table and its collection of paperweights and framed family photos.

Sinclair tried to get between the knight and the dragon. "Saint George," he said in a voice that rang with authority, though it was no more than a whisper. "Might I suggest that you conquer this terrifying serpent outdoors? Things are likely to get broken in the fierce struggle between man and beast."

The first boy bowed gallantly and pointed his sword at Jane. "Fair maid, I've come to rescue you from your tower."

Jane giggled. "Thank you, Sir Fitz, but I am quite happy up here."

Refusing to be upstaged by his twin brother, the other boy growled and circled around a leather chair and ottoman, a writing desk, and a globe on a stand in order to position himself directly under the ladder. "If you don't give me all of your gold, then I'll eat you!" he snarled and held out his hand rakes.

Doing her best to appear frightened, Jane clutched at her chest. "Please, oh fearsome and powerful dragon. have no gold. In fact, my castle is falling apart around me. I was just wishing for a fairy godmother to float down and—"

"There aren't any fairies in this story!" the dragon interrupted crossly. "Fairies are for girls."

"Yeah," the knight echoed indignantly.

Jane knew she had offended her six-year-old sons, but before she could make amends, her eye fell on the ruler in Fitz's hands and an idea struck her.

"Fitz, Hem, you are my heroes!" she cried, hurrying down the ladder.

The boys exchanged befuddled glances. "We are?" They spoke in unison, as they so often did.

"But I'm supposed to be a monster," Hem objected.

Jane touched his cheek. "And you've both been so convincing that you can go straight to the kitchen and tell Mrs. Hubbard that I've given my permission for you both to have an extra piece of chocolate-dipped short-bread at tea this afternoon."

Their gray eyes grew round with delight, but then Fitz whispered something in Hem's ear. Pushing back his salad bowl helm, he gave his mother a mournful look. "Mrs. Hubbard won't believe us. She'll tell us that story about the boy who cried wolf again."

"I'll write a note," Jane said. The boys exchanged high-fives as she scribbled a few lines on an index card.

"Shall I tuck this under one of your scales, Mr. Dragon?" She shoved the note into the pocket of Hem's raincoat. "Now run along. Sinclair and I have a party to plan."

Sinclair waited for the boys to leave before seating himself at his desk chair. He uncapped a fountain pen and held it over a clean notepad. "A party, Miss Jane?"

Jane flounced in the chair across from him and rubbed her palm over the cover of the small book in her hands. "This is Agatha Christie's Death on the Nile."

"Are we having a Halloween party then?" Sinclair asked. "With pharaohs and mummies and such?" He furrowed his shaggy brows. "Did the boys' getups influence your decision?"

"Not just a costume party. Think bigger." Jane hugged the book to her chest with one hand and gestured theatrically with the other. "An entire week of murder and mayhem. We'll have a fancy dress ball and award prizes to those who most closely emulate their favorite fictional detective. Just think," she continued, warming to her idea. "We'll have Hercule Poirot, Sherlock Holmes, Sam Spade, Lord Peter Wimsey, Nick and Nora Charles, Brother Cadfael, Miss Marple, and so on. We'll have readings and skits and teas and banquets. We'll have mystery scavenger hunts and trivia games! Imagine it, Sinclair."

He grimaced. "I'm trying, Miss Jane, but it sounds like an awful lot of hubbub and work. And for what purpose?"

"Money," Jane said simply. "Storyton Hall will be bursting at the seams with paying guests. They'll have the time of their lives and will go home and tell all of their friends how wonderful it was to stay at the nation's only resort catering specifically to readers. We need to let the world know that while we're a place of peace and tranquility, we also offer excitement and adventure."

Sinclair fidgeted with his bow tie again. "Miss Jane, forgive me for saying so, but I believe our guests are interested in three things: comfort, quiet, and good food. I'm not certain they're interested in adventure."

"Our readers aren't sedentary," Jane argued. "I've seen them playing croquet and lawn tennis. I've met them on the hiking and horseback riding trails. I've watched them row across the lake in our little skiffs and walk into Storyton Village. Why wouldn't they enjoy a weekend filled with mystery, glamour, and entertainment?"

The carriage clock on Sinclair's desk chimed three times. "Perhaps you should mention the proposal to your great-aunt and -uncle over tea?"

Jane nodded in agreement. "Brilliant idea. Aunt Octavia is most malleable when she has a plate piled high with scones and lemon cakes. Thank you, Sinclair!" She stood up, walked around the desk, and kissed him lightly on the cheek.

He touched the spot where his skin had turned a rosy shade of pink. "You're welcome, Miss Jane, though I don't think I was of much help."

"You're a librarian," she said on her way out. "To me, that makes you a bigger hero than Saint George, Sir William Wallace, and all of the Knights of the Round

Table put together."

"I love my job," Jane heard Sinclair say before she closed the door.

Jane turned in the opposite direction of the main elevator and headed for the staircase at the other end of a long corridor carpeted in a lush crimson. She was accustomed to traveling a different route than the paying guests of Storyton Hall's guests. Like the rest of the staff, Jane moved noiselessly through a maze of narrow passageways, underground tunnels, dim stairways, attic accesses, and hidden doors in order to be as unobtrusive as possible.

Storyton had fifty bedrooms, eleven of which were on the main floor. And even though Jane's great-aunt and -uncle were in their late seventies, they preferred to remain in their third-story suite of apartments, which included their private library and cozy sitting room, where her aunt liked to spend her evenings reading.

Trotting down a flight of stairs, Jane paused to straighten her skirt before entering the main hallway. Along the wood-paneled walls hung with gilt-framed mirrors, brass sconces, and valuable oil paintings in ornate frames. Massive oak doors stood open, inviting guests to wile away the hours reading in the Jane Austen Parlor, the Ian Fleming Lounge, the Isak Dinesen Safari Room, the Daphne Du Maurier Morning Room, and so on. There was also a Beatrix Potter Playroom for children, but that was located on the basement level as most of the guests preferred not to hear the shrieks and squeals of children when they were trying to lose themselves in a riveting story.

Jane greeted every guest with a "hello" and a smile though her mind was focused on other things. She made a mental checklist as she walked. The door handles need polishing. A lightbulb's gone out by the entrance to Shakespeare's Theater. Eliza needs to stop putting goldenrod in the flower vases. There's pollen on all the tables, and half the guests are sneezing.

She'd almost reached the sunporch when the tiny speakers mounted along the crown molding in the main hallway began to play a recording of bells chiming. Jane glanced at her watch. It was exactly three o'clock.

"Oh, it's teatime!" a woman examining an attractive still life of cherry blossoms exclaimed. Taking the book from a man sitting in one of the dozens of wing chairs lining the hall, she gestured for him to get to his feet. "Come on, Bernard! I want to be the first one in today."

Jane knew there was slim chance of that happening. Guests began congregating at the door of the Agatha Christie Tearoom at half past two. Bobbing her head at the eager pair, she walked past the chattering men, women, and children heading to tea and arrived at the back terrace to find her great-aunt and -uncle seated at a round table with the twins. The table was covered with a snowy white cloth, a vase stuffed with pink peonies, and her aunt's Wedgwood tea set.

"There you are, dear!" Aunt Octavia lifted one of her massive arms and waved regally. Octavia was a very large, very formidable woman. She adored food and loathed exercise. As a result, she'd steadily grown in circumference over the decades and showed no predisposition toward changing her habits, much to her doctor's consternation.

As Jane drew closer, she noticed a rotund tuxedo cat nestled on Aunt Octavia's expansive lap. The feline, who often took tea with the family, had arrived at Storyton Hall during a thunderstorm the previous spring. The twins had discovered the tiny, shivering, half-starved kitten in a corner of the garage, and assuming it was female because of its long eyelashes and stunning gold eyes, named the pathetic creature Miss Muffet. The local veterinarian later informed them that not only was Miss Muffet a male, but judging from the size of his paws, was likely to grow into a very large cat. By this time, everyone had gotten used to calling the cat Miss Muffet. The twins insisted the name be altered to preserve the cat's dignity and so Miss Muffet became Muffet Cat.

Muffet Cat had the run of the resort. He came and went as he pleased, darting through doorways between the feet of startled guests and indulgent staff members. During the day, he vacillated between hunting, napping on the sun porch, and begging for treats, but he spent every night with Aunt Octavia. For half a year, the twins complained that Muffet Cat was a traitor. They claimed they'd rescued him from certain death and he owed them his allegiance, but Muffet Cat merely tolerated them. Aunt Octavia was the center of his feline universe.

"You can't command a cat's affections," Aunt Octavia had explained to the boys. "Muffet Cat prefers the gentler sex. He's a very intelligent animal and knows that he only has to gaze up at a lady with those big, yellow eyes and she feels compelled to feed him a tasty morsel or two."

It was true. Muffet Cat was so perfected this plaintive look that he'd gone from an emaciated kitten to a portly cat within a matter of months.

As Jane took a seat at the table, Muffet Cat opened his eyes into slits, licked a dot of cream from his whiskers, and went back to sleep.

"Hello, everyone," Jane said as she put her napkin on her lap. This was the only time during the day in which he would sit in view of the guests. Very few people noticed the Steward family gathering for tea, being far too busy filling their own plates with sandwiches, scones, cookies, and cakes inside the main house.

Fitz plucked her sleeve. "Mom, can I have another lemon cake?" He glanced at his brother. "Hem too?"

"Fitzgerald Steward," Aunt Octavia said in a low growl. "You've already had enough for six boys. So has Hemingway. Let your mother pour herself some tea before you start demanding seconds. And you should say 'may I,' not 'can I.'"

Nodding solemnly, Fitz sat up straight in his chair and cleared his throat. Doing his best to sound like an English aristocrat, he said, "Madam, may we please have another cake?"

This time, the question was directed at Aunt Octavia. Before she could answer, Hem piped up in a Cockney accent, "Please, mum. We're ever so 'ungry."

Aunt Octavia burst out laughing and passed the platter of sweets. "Incorrigible," she said and put a wrinkled hand over Jane's. "Are you going to the village after tea? Mabel called to say that my new dress is ready and I can't wait to see it. Bright fuchsia with sequins and brown leopard spots. Can you imagine?"

Jane could. Her great-aunt wore voluminous house-dresses fashioned from the most exotic prints and the boldest colors available. She ordered bolts of cloth from an assortment of catalogs and had Mabel Wimberly, a talented seamstress who lived in Storyton Village, sew the fabric into a garment she could slip over her head. Each dress had to come complete with several pockets as Aunt Octavia walked with the aid of a rhinestone-studded cane and liked to load her pockets with gum, hard candy, pens, a notepad, bookmarks, a nail file, treats for Muffet Cat, and other miscellanea. Today, she wore a black and lime zebra-striped dress and a black sunhat decorated with ostrich feathers.

In marked contrast to Aunt Octavia's flamboyant attire, Uncle Aloysius dressed like the country gentleman he was. His slacks and shirt were perfectly pressed, and he always had a handkerchief peeking from the pocket of his suit. The only deviation from this conservative ensemble was his hat. Aloysius wore his fishing hat, complete with hooks, baits, and flies, all day long. He even wore it to church, and Aunt Octavia was forever reminding him to remove it before the service got under way. Some of the staff whispered that he wore the hat to bed as well, but Jane didn't believe it. After all, several of the hooks looked rather sharp.

"What sandwiches did Mrs. Hubbard make today?" she asked her great-uncle.

He patted his flat stomach. Uncle Aloysius was as tall and slender as his wife was squat and round. He was all points and angles to her curves and rolls. Despite their physical dissimilarities and the passage of multiple decades, the two were still very much in love. Jane's great-uncle liked to tell people that he was on a fifty-five-year honeymoon. "My darling wife will tell you that the egg salad and chive is the best," he said. "I started with the brie, watercress, and walnut." He handed Jane the plate of sandwiches and a pair of silver tongs. "That was lovely, but not as good as the fig and goat cheese."

"In that case, I'll have one of each." Jane helped herself to the diminutive sandwiches. "And a raisin scone." Her gaze alighted on the jar of preserves near Aunt Octavia's elbow. "Is that Mrs. Hubbard's blackberry jam?"

"Yes, and it's magnificent. But don't go looking for the Devonshire cream. Muffet Cat and I ate every last dollop." Her great-aunt sat back in her chair, stroked Muffet Cat's glossy fur, and studied Jane. "You've got a spark about you, my girl. Care to enlighten us as to why you have a skip in your step and a twinkle in your eye?"

Jane told her great-aunt and -uncle about her Murder and Mayhem Week idea.

Uncle Aloysius leaned forward and listened without interruption, nodding from time to time. Instantly bored by the topic, Fitz and Hem scooted back their chairs and resumed their knight and dragon personas by skirmishing a few feet from the table until Aunt Octavia shooed them off.

"Go paint some seashells green," she told Hem. "You

can't be a decent dragon without scales. We have an entire bucket of shells in the craft closet."

"What about me?" Fitz asked. "What else do I need to be a knight?"

Aunt Octavia examined him closely. "A proper knight needs a horse. Get a mop and paint a pair of eyes on the handle."

Without another word, the twins sprinted for the basement stairs. Jane saw their sandy heads disappear and grinned. Her aunt had encouraged her to play similar games when she was a child, and it gave her a great deal of satisfaction to see her sons following in her footsteps.

"Imagination is more important than knowledge," was Aunt Octavia's favorite quote, and she repeated it often. She said it again now and then waved for Jane to continue.

Throughout the interruption, Uncle Aloysius hadn't taken his eyes off Jane. When she'd finished outlining her plan, he rubbed the white whiskers on his chin and gazed out across the wide lawn. "I like your idea, my dear. I like it very much. We can charge our guests a special weekly rate. And by special, I mean higher. We'd have to ask a pretty penny for the additional events because I expect we'll need to hire extra help."

"But do you think it will work?"

"I do indeed. It's quite splendid." He smiled. "In fact, it could be the start of a new tradition. Mystery buffs in October, Western readers in July, fantasy fans for May Day."

"A celebration of romance novels for Valentine's!" Aunt Octavia finished with a sweep of her arm.

Uncle Aloysius grabbed hold of his wife's hand and planted a kiss on her palm. "It's Valentine's Day all year long with you, my love."

Watching her great aunt and uncle exchange tender looks, Jane felt a familiar stab of pain. It was during moments like these that she missed her husband most. She'd been a widow for six years and had never been able to think of William Elliot without a pang of sorrow and agony. While her great-uncle and -aunt exchanged whispered endearments, Jane wondered if ten years would be enough time to completely heal the hole in her heart left by her husband's passing.

"Jane? Are you gathering wool?" Aunt Octavia asked.

Shaking off her melancholy, Jane reached for the teapot and poured herself a nice cup of Earl Grey. "I'm afraid I was. Sorry."

"No time for drifting off," Uncle Aloysius said. "There's much to be done to prepare for this Murder and Mayhem Week of yours. And might I say . . ." He paused to collect himself, and Jane knew that he was about to pay her a compliment. Her uncle was always very deliberate when it came to words of praise or criticism. "Your dedication to Storyton Hall does the Steward name proud. I couldn't have asked for a more devoted heir."

Jane thanked him, drank the rest of her tea, and went into the manor house through the kitchen. She tarried for a moment to tell the staff how delicious the tea service was and then walked down the former servants' passage to her small, cozy office.

Sitting behind her desk, Jane flexed her fingers over her computer keyboard and began to type a list of possible events, meals, and decorating ideas for the Murder and Mayhem Week. Satisfied that Storyton Hall's future guests would have a wide range of activities and dining choices during the mystery week, she set about composing a newsletter announcing the dates and room rates. She made the special events appear even more enticing by inserting colorful stock photos of bubbling champagne glasses, people laughing, and couples dancing at a costume ball. She also included the book covers of popular mystery novels from the past century as well as tantalizing photographs of Storyton's most mouth-watering dinner and dessert buffets.

"They'll come in droves," she said to herself, absurdly pleased by the end result of the newsletter. "Uncle Aloysius is right. If this event is a resounding success, we can add more and more themed events over the course of the year. Then we'll be able to fix this old pile of stones until it's just like it was when crazy Walter Egerton Steward had it dismantled, brick by brick, and shipped across the Atlantic. We'll restore the folly and the hedge maze and the orchards." Her eyes grew glassy and she gazed off into the middle distance. "It'll be as he dreamed it would be. An English estate hidden away in the wilds of the Virginia mountains. An oasis for book lovers. A reader's paradise amid the pines."

She reread the newsletter once more, searching for typos or grammatical errors and, finding none, saved the document. She then opened a new e-mail message and typed "newsletter recipients" in the address line. It gave her a little thrill to know that thousands of people would soon read about Storyton Hall's first annual Murder and Mayhem Week.

After composing a short e-mail, Jane hit Send, releasing her invitation into the world. Within seconds, former guests, future guests, and her newspaper and magazine contacts would catch a glimpse of what promised to be an unforgettable seven days. Tomorrow, she'd order print brochures to be mailed to the people on her contact list who preferred a more old-fashioned form of communication.

I'll have contacted thousands of people by the end of the week, Jane thought happily. *Thousands of potential guests. Thousands of lovely readers.*

Closing the open windows on her screen, Jane found herself staring at one of the book covers she'd used for the newsletter. It was Agatha Christie's *Body in the Li-*

brary, and this version from 1960 featured the silhouette of a woman standing in front of shelves of colorful books. Her hands were raised in an effort to fend off an attacker, but the assailant's hands were almost at her throat. The woman's demise was clearly imminent.

"Yes, I'm sure they're lovely people. Each and every one," Jane murmured firmly. "We'll have no scenes bearing any resemblance to this cover. After all, this is a work of fiction."

"Honestly, if you're given the choice between Armageddon or tea, you don't say 'what kind of tea?'"
—**Neil Gaiman**, *author*

Excerpt from
THE BUSY WOMAN'S GUIDE TO MURDER
A Charlotte Adams Mystery
by Mary Jane Maffini

The wind was swirling surplus snow as I trotted up the walkway to Dr. Partridge's house for the second time. It was yet another trip out in the bone-chilling winter that just wouldn't quit. I was hoping that Lydia Johnson was still there. The walkway had been shoveled since my earlier visit and the downstairs lights were glowing warmly.

She answered the door and looked surprised. I took the initiative. I handed her the gift of Kristee's black-and-white fudge, in its distinctive black box with the shiny sheer white ribbon. "I know you are having a tough time, but can you help me, Lydia?"

I had correctly gauged that this was a woman who loved to be helpful. "Of course, come in. I'm glad of the company. I've been going crazy waiting for word and I've been trying to keep busy." Her eyes were still rimmed in pink, but keeping busy had obviously helped.

I stepped into the hallway. Something delicious was cooking, stew perhaps, and there was a faint whiff of fresh bread.

"I'm keeping busy," she said. "I've decided to be optimistic and make his favorite meals and fill up the freezer. It's—"

"A good idea," I said. "This won't take long."

"Take all the time you want. Do you like living room or kitchen? I have to check my soup."

"I like kitchens. Especially if someone has been cooking in them."

That earned me a weak smile and soon I was sitting in the bright kitchen and inhaling the aromas of soup and what turned out to be rolls.

She bustled about and produced some hot tea and a plate of rolls with butter and a choice of cheddar, or strawberry jam. "I put up the jam myself. He likes it."

"So do I."

"I'm not sure how I can help you, but I'm glad you dropped in."

The truth is the best option. I gave it a shot. "There have been some incidents in town that appear to be connected with bullying incidents that took place at St. Jude's High School about fourteen years ago."

"Fourteen years ago? Sam was just finished setting up his practice in Woodbridge not long before that. He came here because of his wife, you know."

"I didn't know."

"She was a physician, doing a residency at Woodbridge General. He followed her, but he had to start all over building up clients."

"Sometimes it's good to start over," I said. "It certainly was for me."

"And it would have been for him too, if Janelle had lived. They bought this house together. She hired me first so they could have some of the comforts of home even though they were both slogging away long hours. She was a very thoughtful person and the love of his life. I think that's why he stays here, rattling around in this place. He can never leave it. It's a long time for a man to be alone."

This was a fascinating glimpse into Dr. Partridge's life, but it was off topic for me. "I was hoping he could tell me about the bullies and the outlook for them."

She straightened up and pursed her lips. "He'd never

talk about his patients."

"I know that. And rightly so, but I wanted more general information. I need to know if a bully can ever truly change. One of the—I guess I could say guilty parties—is now volunteering with very vulnerable people and I'm very worried about that. Also one of the bully's earlier victims seems to be falling apart. I was hoping for advice on how to help her. So I urgently needed to talk to Dr. Partridge."

"I am sure he would have helped."

"This accident of his troubles me."

"Of course, it's tragic. Beyond tragic."

"And it could be convenient for someone."

Her teacup crashed onto the saucer. "What? Who could find something like that convenient?"

"Perhaps one of those bullies he treated." I didn't say perhaps the victim. I hated the idea of Mona being guilty, but while I had to face up to it, I could keep it to myself in this case.

"But why?"

"Because people are dying. There have been several hit-and-runs in Woodbridge, resulting in three deaths. You must have heard about them."

She turned even paler.

I pressed my point. "The people involved are connected with this bullying business. I don't believe these are accidents, although the police seem to. I am sure Dr. Partridge would figure that out. I don't know if the guilty party might have wanted to make sure he was—Lydia? Are you all right?"

She was swaying in her chair, her face now white as the porcelain cup, her eyes staring.

"What is it?" I said. "Do you know something about this?"

She shuddered as she spoke. "Hit-and-run deaths?"

"Yes. That's right."

"Oh my God."

"What is it? The hit-and-runs?"

"Janelle."

"His wife?" I was desperate to stay on topic and didn't want to digress to discuss the tragedy of the long-dead wife.

She nodded. "Didn't you know?"

"Know what?"

"That's how she died." Her hands shook. "This is so shocking."

I couldn't believe my ears. "He never mentioned it."

"He wouldn't. He still finds it hard to talk about it. She got home late from the hospital one night and was hit just as she got out of the car. The driveway was being repaired and she had to park the car across the street. It was a dark night, raining, but the driver must have known he'd hit her. How could he not have? Sam found her body hours later when he went out searching for her. That was the end of their storybook marriage."

I shivered.

Lydia sputtered. "That driver left her for dead on the road. I am still so angry about that."

I actually felt a pounding in my ears. This explained Dr. Partridge's odd reaction to my questions. "Hit-and-run" would have triggered powerful emotions in him.

Thinking about Dr. Partridge, I'd tuned out Lydia who was still sounding off. "He should have been caught and put on trial. But the police were quite useless."

"Tell me about it. I can't get them to listen to me at all. Do you mean they never found the person who killed Mrs. Partridge?"

"She was also Dr. Partridge."

"Sorry, of course."

"That doesn't matter. I don't know why I snapped at you. It's just so upsetting that's all. And no. They never found the man who did it. He's probably having a happy comfortable life while Janelle lies cold and dead for four-teen years and Sam has had his life ruined."

"There's something—"

She cut me off, taking my hand. Tears were welling in her eyes again. "Talking about these hit-and-runs triggers all these memories and feelings. I can't believe it. Is he doing it on purpose? Could it be the same man? I suppose it couldn't be."

I took a deep breath. "You keep saying 'he' for the driver. Is there any reason to think it was a man?"

She shuddered. After a long pause she said, "It never entered my mind that a woman could do something like that. Do you think it's possible for a woman to deliberately smash into someone with a vehicle? Such violence."

I understood her feelings. It would have to be someone who enjoyed inflicting pain and misery for the victims and the families. "I do. Horrible, but possible. I believe it is a woman who's committing these hit-and-runs. And I am beginning to wonder if it was a girl who ran down Dr. Janelle Partridge all those years ago."

She turned pale. "A girl? But why?"

"I don't know for sure, but Dr. Partridge saw at least one person who was involved in the bullying episodes."

"That might make sense. You know something strange? The night Janelle died, she was driving Sam's car. It was a snowy night and his tires were better than hers. She was bundled up. Perhaps someone thought they were getting rid of him."

"That makes sense. And that's why I am here. I didn't even know how his wife died, but I was pretty sure that Dr. Partridge was not the type of person to mix up his medications. Do you disagree with that?"

Her mouth hung open. She closed it and shook her head violently. "No. No he wasn't the type to do that. He was very methodical. Are you suggesting that someone—

I don't even know how anyone else could have done

that."

"But I am convinced that someone did. I also know that the police won't believe me. So I am hoping for help from you."

"Anything I can do. It's horrifying to consider that someone would do that to Sam, but it makes more sense. I don't believe he made that mistake himself."

"Exactly."

"But I would have known if someone was in the house last night. There was no sign of anyone breaking in and we are the only two people with a key."

"I have a glimmer of an idea. The medications didn't have to be mixed up. Someone just needed to ensure that he had an overdose."

She blinked. "But how could someone do that?"

"Could someone have come by here the night before?"

"I don't know. I was out at my bridge club. Sam was already in bed when I came home at about ten."

"Do you live here?"

"Yes. I get my accommodation and Sam gets a bit of TLC. I have a separate entrance and we both guard our privacy, but it's nice to have a bit of company. At any rate ten was a bit early even for him, although he gets up at dawn. The lights were all out except the hall light, which he always leaves on for me."

"Is there any way for you to know if he had clients last night?"

She shrugged. "He rarely sees them in the night, but he has an appointment book. It's in his office." She stood up, resolute. "Let's go."

I followed her down the hall and into a large office that would have originally been a dining room. The cool blue walls were lined with books, neatly organized. The large teak desk was as I might have expected; neat with small in-basket and a twin out-basket. The in-basket was empty, I noticed admiringly. The out-basket held a few documents.

Lydia said, "It should be right there."

"Where?"

"On his desk. He leaves it right there every day. Where is it?" She checked the out-basket, then whirled around as if expecting to find it on one of the two comfortable chairs or lying on the plush oriental carpet. "That is very strange. Someone must have taken it. Unless it's upstairs in his bedroom." She hesitated and then made straight for the staircase and upstairs in good time. I followed her, hoping to get away with it.

At the door, she said, "I haven't let myself come back in here. I suppose I'll have to face it sooner or later."

In the bedroom, the bed was still made but rumpled, as if someone had slept on top of the covers. A glass of water had been knocked from the bedside table onto the floor. A jumble of clothing lay on the floor—pants, shirt, hand-knit brown sweater, socks, and underwear. Nothing else was out of order to my mind. There was no sign of an appointment book.

"Understandable," I said. "My guess is that somebody didn't want anyone to find out that she had been to see him."

"That would explain it," she said, frowning, as she bent to pick up a pair of pants and a shirt. "Now that's odd."

"Let me guess. He always hangs everything up before he goes to bed."

"And his laundry's in the hamper. I don't think Sam's clothes would have ever touched the floor before this. I've never had to pick them up. What does it mean?"

I could feel the answer explode in my head. I knew what it would mean for me. "It means that he was drugged before he went upstairs. Someone slipped him an extra dose of whatever medications he was taking."

"But how?"

"Perhaps they slipped something into his coffee or tea."

"Oh, coffee. He was always drinking coffee."

"And he took it very sweet."

She smiled. "Three sugars in each one."

"So perhaps he wouldn't notice the taste. Did you find a cup or a mug?"

"Mug. He always used a mug. Oh my heavens. I washed them up when I saw them."

"Them?"

"Yes. There were two in the living room. If there was something in one of them, that would be gone now."

"You had no way of knowing. He would have been extremely groggy by the time he got up here and that might explain the clothes on the floor. It would have been all he could have done to get on the bed. He must have knocked over the glass of water then and fell and hit his head trying to get it. Or maybe he had been reaching for the phone to call for help and lost consciousness."

"Who could have done such a terrible thing?"

"Like I said before, it's someone with a lot to lose, perhaps. I'm guessing it was a bully turned murderer who was afraid that Dr. Partridge would reveal her secret."

A small voice in the back of my head said, don't forget Mona.

About The Authors

Ellery Adams is the author of three New York Times best-selling series, including the Book Retreat mysteries, the Books by the Bay Mysteries, and the Charmed Pie Shoppe Mysteries. In addition to these, she also writes three ebook series. These include The Supper Club mysteries, The Hope Street mysteries, and the Molly Appleby Antiques and Collectibles mysteries. For more killer reads, please visit www.elleryadamsmysteries.com

The immensely popular Booktown Mystery series is what put **Lorraine Bartlett's** pen name Lorna Barrett on the New York Times Bestseller list, but it's her talent—whether writing as Lorna, or L.L. Bartlett, or Lorraine Bartlett—that keeps her in the hearts of her readers. This multi-published, Agatha-nominated author pens the exciting Jeff Resnick Mysteries as well as the acclaimed Victoria Square and Lotus Bay mystery series, and the Tales of Telenia adventure-fantasy series, and has many short stories and novellas to her name(s). Visit her website: http://www.LorraineBartlett.com

While others girls dreamed of dating guys like Brad Pitt, **Duffy Brown** longed to take Sherlock Holmes to the prom. Today she is a National Bestselling author and conjures up who-done-it stories for Berkley Prime Crime. She has two series, the Consignment Shop Mysteries set in Savannah, and the Cycle Path Mysteries on Mackinac Island. Visit her website at http://www.DuffyBrown.com

Kate Collins is the New York Times bestselling author of the long-running Flower Shop Mystery series. After publishing a series of children's stories, she sold her first historical romantic suspense novel in 1995. Seven romance novels later, she switched to her true love, mysteries. Kate is very proud that The Flower Shop Mystery series was named The Best Continuing Cozy Mystery Series for 2013 by popular online review site Escape with Dollycas. When not growing roots at her computer, Kate loves to garden. Other passions include yoga, travel, decorating, reading, spending time with family and friends, sampling great wines and fine dark chocolate, and enjoying every moment of life. She lives in Northwest Indiana and Key West, Florida. Read about Kate's mysteries, historical romances, and children's anthologies at www.katecollins-books.com

Mary Kennedy is a practicing psychologist and author of the Dream Club and Talk Radio Mysteries, as well as the Hollywood Nights young adult stories. She lives on the East Coast with her husband and seven neurotic cats. Both husband and cats have resisted her attempts to psychoanalyze them, but she remains optimistic. Visit her website at http://www.MaryKennedy.net

Lapsed librarian and former mystery bookstore owner, **Mary Jane Maffini** is the author of thirteen mysteries in three series: The Camilla MacPhee books, The Fiona Silk Capers and the Charlotte Adams mysteries. She's won a number of awards, including an Agatha, for short stories and the fifth Charlotte Adams book, The Busy Woman's Guide to Murder, won the Romantic Times award for best amateur sleuth. As that shadowy figure known as Victoria Abbott, she writes the book collector mysteries with her daughter, the artist and photographer, Victoria Maffini. Find out more at http://www.MaryJane-Maffini.com and http://www.Victoria-Abbott.com

Maggie Sefton is the author of the New York Times bestselling Knitting Mysteries. She was born and raised in northern Virginia and has worked in several careers over the years, from a CPA to a real estate broker in the Rocky Mountain West. However, none of those endeavors could compare with the satisfaction and challenge of creating worlds on paper. She is the mother of four grown daughters, currently scattered around the globe, and resides in the Rocky Mountains of Colorado. Visit her website at http://www.MaggieSefton.com

Leann Sweeney is the author of the Yellow Rose Mysteries, that feature Abby Rose and Yellow Rose Investigations hoping to reunite adoptees with their birth parents in Texas. She also writes the Cats in Trouble Mysteries, featuring quilt maker and cat-rescue sleuth Jillian Hart, set in South Carolina. She lives on a lake in South Carolina with her husband, her dog and two cats. To learn more about Leann and her books, visit her website: http://www.LeannSweeney.com

Recipe Index

THE COZY CHICKS

Made in the USA
Las Vegas, NV
24 February 2024